Battleground Europe

HILL 60

173. A MINE CRATER. HILL 60.

With the continued expansion of the Battleground series a **Battleground Series Club** has been formed to benefit the reader. The purpose of the Club is to keep members informed of new titles and to offer many other reader-benefits. Membership is free and by registering an interest you can help us predict print runs and thus assist us in maintaining the quality and prices at their present levels.

Please call the office 01226 734555, or send your name and address along with a request for more information to:

Battleground Series Club Pen & Sword Books Ltd, 47 Church Street, Barnsley, South Yorkshire S70 2AS

Battleground Europe

HILL 60

Nigel Cave

Series editor
Nigel Cave

LEO COOPER

I dedicate this book to the staff of Talbot House who have looked after pilgrims, including myself, to the Immortal Salient for so many years, carrying on with great commitment the work of Tubby Clayton. In particular I remember with especial affection Ivy and Charlie Swan, wardens during my first stay in 1981; whilst the present permanent staff, Jacques Ryckebosch, Martine Boone, Myriam Herkelbout, Juan Tetaert and Lena Goudeseune have been unfailing in their attention and willingness to help. I have happy memories of a number of wardens, most notably Keith and Winifred Watson, Bert Hill, Irene Waters, Betty Hall and Neville Minas. Mike Lyddiard of Toc H headquarters, has also been a wonderful post dinner conversation companion. Talbot House has become my home on the Salient, and what more could one ask.

First published in 1998, reprinted 2000, 2004
by
LEO COOPER
an imprint of
Pen & Sword Books Limited
47 Church Street, Barnsley, South Yorkshire S70 2AS

ISBN 0 85052 559 4

A CIP record of this book is available
from the British Library

Printed by CPI UK

For up-to-date information on other titles produced under the Leo Cooper imprint, please telephone or write to:

Pen & Sword Books Ltd, FREEPOST, 47 Church Street
Barnsley, South Yorkshire S70 2AS
Telephone 01226 734222

Cover Painting: **Hill 60** by Fred Roe.
By kind permission of the Queen's Royal Surrey Regiment.

CONTENTS

HILL 60 THE SCENE OF BITTER FIGHTING WAS HELD BY GERMAN TROOPS FROM THE 16TH
DECEMBER 1914 TO THE 17TH APRIL 1915 WHEN IT WAS CAPTURED AFTER THE EXPLOSION OF
FIVE MINES BY THE BRITISH 5TH DIVISION. ON THE FOLLOWING 5TH MAY IT WAS
RECAPTURED BY THE GERMAN XV CORPS. IT REMAINED IN GERMAN HANDS UNTIL THE
BATTLE OF MESSINES 7TH JUNE 1917 WHEN AFTER MANY MONTHS OF UNDERGROUND
FIGHTING TWO MINES WERE EXPLODED HERE AND AT THE END OF APRIL 1918 AFTER THE
BATTLES OF THE LYS IT PASSED INTO GERMAN HANDS AGAIN. IT WAS FINALLY RETAKEN BY
BRITISH TROOPS UNDER THE COMMAND OF H.M. KING OF THE BELGIANS ON THE 28TH
SEPTEMBER 1918.
IN THE BROKEN TUNNELS BENEATH THIS ENCLOSURE MANY BRITISH AND GERMAN DEAD
WERE BURIED AND THE HILL IS THEREFORE PRESERVED SO FAR AS NATURE WILL PERMIT IN
THE STATE IN WHICH IT WAS LEFT AFTER THE GREAT WAR.

ACKNOWLEDGEMENTS

Once more, as with all my books, I owe much of the contents of this one to the labours of love that characterises many of the divisional, regimental and battalion histories of the Great War. They were largely designed to ensure that those who were in the various units and formations had a means of reminding themselves of what happened, where they were, what went on and, of course, of their friends, fallen, wounded, crippled and unmarked, at least externally. Time has meant that the survivors are nearly all gone, and the recent great enthusiasm for the study of the war has resulted in copies of these tomes becoming almost unreachably expensive – they now cost something like £80 apiece on average. Their content is often rather uninteresting and bland, but quite frequently there are moving and emotive passages which deserve a better fate than to be confined to the pages of dusty volumes and inaccessible to any but the fortunate few, or in the great war libraries such as that at the Imperial War Museum or the National Army Museum. Therefore I make no apology about making such extensive use of them and can only say that I, at least, am deeply grateful for their legacy in adding flesh to the few physical reminders of the war – apart, that is, from the cemeteries, of that dreadful conflict.

I have a number of personal thanks to make. Richard Brucciani once more made both himself and his plane freely available for me to make another aerial tour of the battlefields; and once more we were blessed with excellent weather to carry out the mission. Colonel Phillip Robinson has been a mine of information on all aspects of tunnelling,

9.2 Howitzer near Ypres in 1917 – an all too familiar landscape. Note the shells, in the right foreground, raised above the muck.

and has produced some superb material with which I have been able to illustrate the work of those men which is forever associated with Hill 60. I am very grateful for all the time and energy he has put in on my behalf. Ralph Whitehead in far away New York state has produced translations of German unit and formation histories, maps and a wealth of photographs, fitting all this into his busy family and business schedule. His contribution has been invaluable in providing some balance to the story of the hill. Steve Shannon proved to be a great professional companion when I spent some months based in Durham, and I am grateful to him for extracts from 13/DLI War Diary – and also for much else besides. I thank Durham County Council for allowing me to reproduce part of these.

Michel Delannoy runs the little café and evocative museum close by Hill 60, and I have enjoyed his hospitality and the facilities he offers on numerous occasions. Please do not leave the area without looking at the splendid collection of material from the war, and the quite horrifying 3D photographs which may be examined through stereoscopic viewers.

I have made innumerable friends in the area around the Salient, in the cafes and the coffee shops; they make a visit here seem like home from home. That is why I have been moved to dedicate this book to the people who work at Talbot House, now and in the past.

Various former pupils have accompanied me on my tours to the site. Mark Fisher has been one, but my especial thanks go to James Congdon who accompanied me in indifferent weather in January to get the photography done. I think he might be unaware that the ulterior motive was a burly set of shoulders to push the car out of the mud, and he came pretty close to being called to exercise his strength when the car threatened to bog down near Larch Wood cemetery.

Colleagues and friends in the Western Front Association have provided encouragement, and more to the point bought the books! Peter Oldham has written an excellent book, *Pill Boxes on the Western Front*, and I am grateful to him and the publishers for allowing me to reproduce the part devoted to the Hill 60 bunker, which always provokes questions and comments.

Finally I would like to pay tribute, once more, for the hard work of the members of the Commonwealth War Graves Commission who work in the area covered by this book. Hill 60 is kept in wonderful condition, emulating the care and attention devoted to the cemeteries around and about. They, more than anyone else, carry the torch of remembrance.

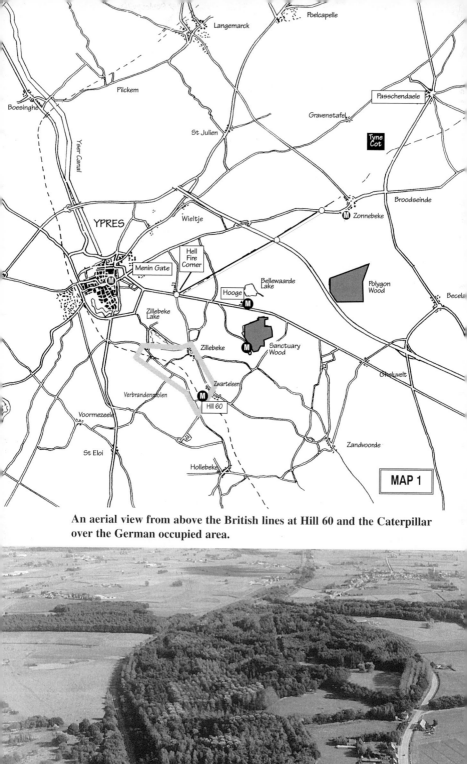

MAP 1

An aerial view from above the British lines at Hill 60 and the Caterpillar over the German occupied area.

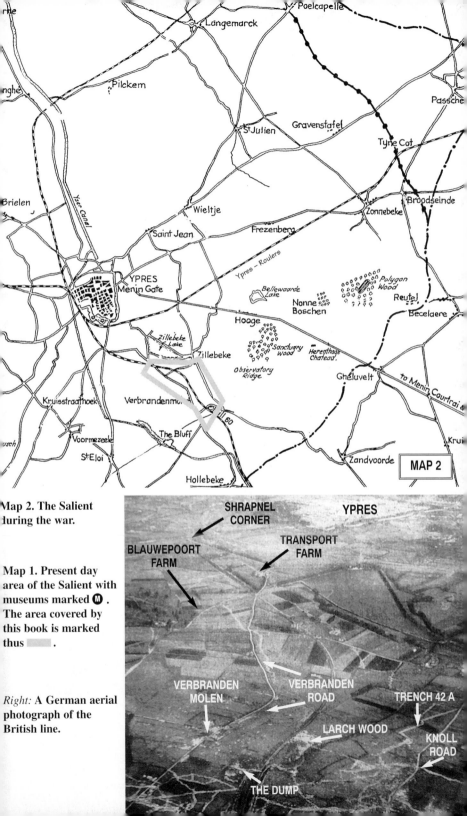

MAP 2

Map 2. The Salient during the war.

Map 1. Present day area of the Salient with museums marked Ⓜ. The area covered by this book is marked thus [   ].

Right: A German aerial photograph of the British line.

YPRES

SHRAPNEL CORNER

BLAUWEPOORT FARM

TRANSPORT FARM

VERBRANDEN MOLEN

VERBRANDEN ROAD

TRENCH 42 A

LARCH WOOD

KNOLL ROAD

THE DUMP

INTRODUCTION

Hill 60 is now a quiet, pockmarked piece of land that is maintained in as an unaltered state as is practicable by the Commonwealth War Graves Commission. Nature is kept under control primarily by the use of sheep. It is ironic that 'sheep may safely graze' where once havoc was a daily occurrence. It is hard to believe, and even harder to imagine, what it must have been like to be here during almost all of the war. In 1914 it was a question of desperately trying to cling on, and prevent the hordes of Germans breaking through the thin Anglo-French line that protected not only Ypres but, more significantly, the road to the French coast and the British supply lines to its 'contemptibly little' force on the continent. In 1915 an attempt was made to secure the artificial prominence created from the spoil of the railway line to its south which had been lost by the weakened French forces that held this sector in December 1914. This involved the use of mines, amongst the earliest fired by the British. The bitter fighting of April 1915 resulted in the winning of four VCs. But just as the British were determined to capture the hill, the Germans were determined to get it back, and the following month saw them wresting control back once more, an attack forever allied with the first use of poison gas against the British.

The Germans had gained what they wanted, that is the dominating view that Hill 60 provided over great swathes of the British line and in particular into Ypres itself. They were quite happy to sit here in this superior position, though there was fighting on the periphery of the position in the attack of 2 June 1916 against the Canadians who held the line from just north of Hooge to just south of St Eloi. This attack centred on the area around Sanctuary Wood and Mount Sorel, with a later attack launched against Hooge.

In 1917 Hill 60 was once more blasted by large British mines, in

View from site of Trench 38 toward Ypres.

this case as part of the June Messines Offensive. The mines here were at the northernmost point of the attack, and the violent blast, accompanied by the massive artillery bombardment, swept the Germans a considerable distance to the east. But they were not to be denied, and in the Lys Offensive of spring 1918 they not only captured the hill but came close to taking Ypres, and all that entailed. It was not until September 1918 that the Germans were finally removed.

This book covers a very small site – what was described by Billy Congreve as an area no bigger than the centre of Trafalgar Square. It is doubtful if there will be another book in the series that will concern itself with such a tiny patch of land. Yet it became a well known and feared name for most of 1915, along with a few others in the Salient, such as Hooge, the Bluff and St Eloi. In the post war years this was a place which drew many visitors. For in those years between the wars, when my father first came on a pilgrimage with his father, a veteran of the Great War, there were preserved trenches and underground dugouts to visit. Indeed on my first visit to the Salient, with my father in 1968, we made a bee-line for Hill 60. Alas, these remnants have long since gone, and all that now remains is the Hill itself and the basic, but fascinating, museum in the nearby Queen Victoria's Rifles café. Perhaps it is as well for, unlike the great jostling masses that turn up by the coach load to the museum and trenches at Hill 62 on the edge of Sanctuary Wood, this is a much quieter spot and allows that much more scope for individual reflection.

The purpose of this guide is to help the visitor to understand the basics of the larger actions that took place on and around the Hill and to know something of the individuals and formations that fought so bravely and resolutely. The tour section is, in fact, simplicity itself, as there is such a tiny enclosure; but the walk will give an insight into the routes followed by the men to and from the trenches, the difficulties they faced and the importance of the topography. The cemeteries that are included tell their own evocative story.

ADVICE TO TOURERS

To make the most of your visit I would recommend that you read this book through before you commence your touring so that you can get a firm idea of the Hill and what took place there before looking at the ground.

When touring the Salient the obvious place to stay is in Ypres, the town which is associated more than any other with the British armies of the Great War. The visitor has only a short drive from the Channel Ports to Ypres (or Ieper as it is known in this Flemish part of Belgium, and this is the name usually found on signposts). Just over an hour after leaving Calais one can expect to be enjoying the wonders of the town's one way system.

The information and tourist office, which is to be found at the east end of the Cloth Hall, produces a sizeable list of places to stay, from very comfortable hotels through to bed and breakfasts, the latter mainly to be found in the surrounding villages. Although there are not the number of British owned establishments as are to be found on the Somme, there are a few, the most accessible of which is The Shell Hole. This is situated at the further end of d'Hondstraat (number 54-56) from the Grote Markt, or main square. Besides offering en suite rooms John Woolsgrove, the proprietor, offers an excellent English breakfast and a bar/café whilst there is the very considerable bonus in

The Square at Ypres pictured in November 1916.

TAYLOR LIBRARY

the adjoining building of his excellent bookshop and collection of artefacts, maps, contemporary postcards and the like. He can be contacted on (00 32) 57 20 87 88. The rebuilt Hooge chateau (not on the site of the pre-war one, which is now in the pleasure park next door) is also a hotel with good en suite facilities and a restaurant, and might be to the taste of those who want to be right on the battlefield and indeed the hotel grounds incorporate the infamous Hooge Crater (see my *Sanctuary Wood and Hooge* in this series).

There are plenty of restaurants and cafes around the Grote Markt, and parking is not usually particularly difficult. However you should be warned that Saturday is market day and you would be well advised to keep clear of Ypres until 1 pm. Cafes and restaurants like the Trumpet and the Old Tom offer excellent value meals. For those who want to eat on the hoof, there is a useful supermarket opposite the south west side of St Martin's, the main church (not, technically, a cathedral, though easily impressive enough to be one). On the road leading up to the Menin Gate there is a well stocked delicatessen with a very helpful staff.

The people of Ypres are helpful and their linguistic skills put most of us to shame. In the town most people in the shops will speak a sufficiency of English for practical purposes. Indeed, people seem to be more willing to use English than French. In the rural areas, in particular the farms around Hill 60, you might find that Flemish only is spoken; sign language will have to do!

The main museum for the area is the Cloth Hall, a hugely expensive refurbishment of which was completed in 1998. This has not been without controversy, as the museum now has a particular axe to grind, that is peace. Whilst, of course, naturally admirable in itself, there seems to be a danger of moving away from a record of what happened in the past and leaving the gruesome photographs, the artefacts, the tragedy of the surrounding cemeteries and the memorials to hammer home the inordinate cost of conflict and the concomitant human suffering and instead attempting to ram a particular message home. I shall await to see what the museum is like in due course, but remain somewhat sceptical; it will certainly be much larger and much more 'high tech' than its predecessor. The town itself is to be marketed as a town of peace, comparable to Dresden, Hiroshima and Stalingrad.

For those who like their museums old fashioned, then I recommend the one at Sanctuary Wood Hill 62, which still has original trenches (though, naturally, well maintained ones!), and the chaotic but delightful museum attached to the Queen Victoria's Rifles café at Hill

60. There is an excellent museum at Zonnebeke, which has eccentric opening hours which should be checked with the tourist office; whilst a relatively new venture in the former Hooge Chapel is particularly recommended. This museum has some excellent dioramas and a collection of well displayed artefacts, the culmination of which is a dramatic stack of shells positioned in the old entrance.

The most useful map for navigation is in the French Green series, the 1:100000 Lille Dunkirk map, number 2. The most detailed map which is readily available is the 1:50000; this may be obtained, inter alia, from the Tourist Office. There are good 1:25000 maps produced in Belgium, but I have only ever been able to obtain them either through a specialist shop in the UK or direct from the IGN shop in Brussels.

The Commonwealth War Graves Commission has an office in Ypres at 82, Elverdingestraat (about half a mile along the road from St George's Chapel). It is open during working days, and from there you may purchase a Michelin 1:200000 map overprinted with the location of the bulk of the cemeteries (the main exclusion is small plots in communal cemeteries). There are three of these maps, covering most of the old British area of the front; the one required for the Ypres area is 51, Calais Lille Bruxelles. It is also possible to obtain the location of individual burials, but it is essential to have some basic information, such as regiment (and preferably battalion) and possibly the date of death (even the year would help). Readers should know that soldiers' and officers' records are now available at the Public Record Office at Kew, though there may be gaps, mainly as a result of bombing in the

Second World War of the warehousing where they were stored.

The most useful general guide to the area is Major and Mrs Holt's *Ypres Salient*, published by Leo Cooper, Pen and Sword which, besides giving you a very full description of the battle area and various tours, also has an excellent separate map with the principal points of interest marked upon it.

Before setting off from home, ensure that you are adequately insured, and bring your Form E1 11 that provides reciprocal medical care. This form is obtainable from major Post Offices. The Green Card seems to have gone the way of all flesh, but check with your vehicle insurers. You would be strongly advised to ensure that you have a tetanus jab, or that your current one is still effective. There is a lot of rusty old wire and the like, and it is

The Grande Place and Cloth

easy to cut yourself on it.

The following items will be useful. A good pair of stout shoes or walking boots kept in the boot to change into when walking the area is essential; wellingtons will be handy, especially if the intention is to go along the trenches at Hill 62. A good camera, preferably with telephoto lens is essential, along with a notebook to record what and where the photograph taken actually is; a tripod is necessary in many cases if you intend to photograph names on memorials – it is almost inevitable that the names you want will be right at the top of a darkened recess of the Menin Gate or the Tyne Cot Memorial. Binoculars and a compass will help. You will need a small rucksack to carry this lot around, along with a hat (it gets quite chilly in the autumn and winter months) and gloves. You will need suitable cutlery and a mug for your al fresco lunch, and never forget the bottle opener and corkscrew.

The war's physical impact continues to recede with the years, but the weapons of destruction still emerge from the ground. Shells, grenades and the like may be old, but they can still be lethal; a Belgian was killed in Furnes in 1997 examining a grenade. These objects should be left well alone – there is nothing wrong with looking, but please do not touch them.

The tours I have suggested are all along public routes; please do not walk across fields unless the prior permission of the landowner is sought, and be considerate when parking. Be warned that most roads in Belgium have at least one cycle lane and it is an offence to stop on them. It can also lead to the slightly unnerving experience (for example on the road from Shrapnel Corner to Railway Dugouts and beyond) of a car coming at you on one side of the road and a cyclist on what you might think is your side.

Ypres is a beautiful place, especially in the centre which has risen, phoenix-like, from

Lille Gate, Ypres.

the brick strewn wreck to which it was reduced by 1918. In July 1917 Fr Willie Doyle, a chaplain in the 16th (Irish) Division, described moving through it.

In silence, save for the never ceasing roar of the guns and the rumble of the cartwheels, we marched on through the city of the dead, Ypres, not a little anxious, for a shower of shells might come at any minute. Ruin and desolation, desolation and ruin, is the only description I can give of a spot once the pride and glory of Belgium. The hand of war has fallen heavily on the city of Ypres; scarce a stone remains of the glorious cathedral and the equally famous Cloth Hall; the churches, a dozen of them, are piles of rubbish, gone are the convents, the hospitals and the public buildings, and though many of the inhabitants are still there, their bodies lie buried in the ruins of their homes, and the smell of rotting corpses poisons the air. I have seen strange sights in the last two years, but this was the worst of all. Out again by the opposite gate of this stricken spot [the Menin Gate], *which people say was not undeserving of God's chastisement, across the moat and along the road pitted all over with half filled-in shell holes. Broken carts and dead horses, with human*

bones too if one looked, lie on all sides, but one is too weary to think of anything except how many more miles must be covered.

It is hard, when walking around the town, to think that he can be describing the same place.

To get to Hill 60 proceed to the west end of the Grote Markt and, beyond the fountain on your right, follow the road round to the left, which becomes Rijselstraat (Flemish for Lille). Go under the Lille gate, noting on your right as you proceed over the moat the beautifully located Ramparts Cemetery. Continue straight ahead at the roundabout and just before the railway crossing turn left. This crossroad was known as Shrapnel Corner; not as notorious as Hell Fire Corner further to the north, but quite bad enough. Proceed along here for some three miles or so, and you will see a sign (blue lettering on a white background) indicating Hill 60.

HILL 60: THE MAPS

The Moat, Lille Gate and Ramparts Cemetery, Ypres.

Chapter One

THE ATTACK OF 17-21 APRIL 1915

Hill 60 was created, along with two other, lower, features on the other side of the track, the Caterpillar (to the south) and the Dump (to the west), by the spoil excavated when a cutting was put in for the Ypres-Comines railway. Hill 60 got its name from the contour line marking it on the map and the Caterpillar because of its shape; the least impressive in size was the Dump, where the earth was piled up to a point.

On 10 December Hill 60 was captured from the French by the Germans; soon after the British returned to the sector in February 1915 it took over plans to raid the hill, which under the orders of GHQ (General Headquarters of the British Expeditionary Force) became more involved, with the aim of holding it.

British trenches on Hill 60 – March 1915.

> *At the time we sometimes wondered what it was all for, this attack on what was called a 'hill' but which to us at time was merely a system of muddy trenches shell-torn ground, and a haunt of death. The place was practically a cemetery, and hundreds must have been buried on the ground, it proving impossible, when digging trenches, not to disturb some poor fellow in his last long sleep.*
> Lieutenant CWG Ince, Adjutant 2/Duke of Wellington's.

This was to be done in conjunction with a mining operation, which will be dealt with elsewhere.

The Official History[1] expresses doubts about this decision, arguing that because the capture of the hill would create a small salient in the British line, and leave it vulnerable to enfilade fire, in particular from the Caterpillar, that the best policy would have been a raid which would have forced the Germans to garrison it strongly, at the same time leaving them exposed to artillery fire. The alternative would have been a much greater action that would have resulted in the capture of the Caterpillar as well, but this would have been a very difficult operation, not least because of the intervening railway line, and in any case it was doubtful if the British had sufficient resources, especially of artillery, to conduct such an attack successfully. The Germans regarded the hill as of great value as an observation point into Ypres and the British approaches to the front, it is true, but in 1915 they were far better equipped than the British with close support fire, such as trench mortars and grenades.

The attack was to be carried out by 13 Brigade, 5th Division, which consisted of 1/West Kent (1/RWK), 2/KOSB (these to front the attack), 2/Duke of Wellington's in support and Queen Victoria's Rifles (a TA battalion of the London Regiment) and 2/KOYLI in reserve.

See Maps p.109 p.30

At just after 7 pm on 17 April two pairs of mines (the northern pair 2,000 pounds of powder each; the southern pair 2,700) and a single mine, to the south of these, of 500 pounds, were fired at ten second intervals. That under Hill 60 was fired first; the second, to the west of it opposite Trench 38, was fired second, and the third to be fired was opposite Trench 40. A company of 1/RWK and some sappers rushed forward and soon occupied the craters and the remnants of the German positions. The Germans counter-attacked heavily throughout the next couple of nights and days, in the course of which 13 Brigade was relieved successively by the 15th and 14th. In effect, this first phase of the battle was over, but it was merely a lull in the fighting at Hill 60. This stupendously heavy fighting in such a restricted area resulted in the award of four Victoria Crosses.

Alexander Johnston, then commanding the Signal Company of the 5th Division, commented on the events on the hill; his position at a divisonal headquarters in charge of signals meant that he could be kept well abreast of what was going on.[2]

At 7 pm the show began by 3 mines [in fact five, see above] *being sprung under the German trenches on Hill 60: they were most successful as they wrecked the German line and blew up or* buried about 150 Germans. The assault of the hill was then carried out by 1/RWK and 2/KOSB who took the hill without any difficulty and with little loss. Very heavy shelling was opened on both sides: the Germans for one thing had not got their guns registered on what had been their own hill, and anyway shelled behind the line chiefly with a view to catching our reserves and preventing reinforcements coming up. Our people therefore had a short respite in which to dig themselves in , and consolidating their position; the supporting battalions were busy bringing up sandbags etc and digging communication trenches up from our old line to the new. Though there was a lot of heavy firing all through the night, they were able to make good headway both with the front line and with the communication trenches, so that they were better able to resist the very heavy counter-attack which the Germans launched at 5.30 am and which lasted till 7 am. There was very severe fighting, much of it hand to hand and, though we lost pretty heavily, we held on to all the ground gained and inflicted very severe losses on the Germans, a machine gun of ours in particular doing great execution. Hill 60 is an important point as, with it in our possession, a large area of

Group of Officers 1/RWK taken the day before Hill 60. Note in particular, Lieutenant Poland, killed during the German counter attack in the early hours of 18 April. Left to right: **Capt Lynch White,** *commanded troops on Hill for several hours during the battle..* **Lt Poland,** *killed.* **Lt Craston,** *died of wounds.* **Lt Wild,** *wounded.* **Lt Maunder,** *wounded.* **Lt Hilder,** *wounded.* **Lt Liebenrood,** *wounded.* **Lt Bradley, Transport Officer,** *killed at Pilkem.* **Lt Doe,** *wounded.* **Capt Tuff,** *killed on Hill 60.*

country behind our lines is shut out from view of the Germans, who formerly could watch the whole of this tract and got a fine view of many of our trenches.

On 18 April Johnston noted in his diary,

> *At 6 pm the 5th Division made a further attack to round off their new position, which was completely successful: they however had a very bad night of it, as the Germans worried them a great deal with hand grenades and bombs, which our fellows could not reply to as our supply of hand grenades soon gave out! So typical of the way we wage war, never properly prepared. However they held on but had a bad time.*

On 20 April he writes more on Hill 60, having heard reports from first hand survivors of the earlier fighting there.

> *It seems that at first we occupied a T shaped sap in front of the newly gained ground: unfortunately some officers who went forward to reconnoitre were knocked out there, the importance of this sap possibly was not realised, but anyway it was evacuated, the Germans got in there with grenades etc and made a bit of our line quite untenable: our people had to withdraw a bit and lie out in the open on the reverse slope of the hill for most of the day: hence a second attack that evening, which was successful.*

Later in the evening of the 20th he went up to Scherpenberg (a hill some seven or eight miles west of Hill 60).

> *It was a wonderful sight from up there, looking over an enormous length of line which was marked out almost by the flares which both sides were throwing up and by the flashes of the guns and the bursts of the shells. There was obviously another tremendous struggle about Hill 60.*

On his return to his divisional headquarters at Reninghelst he was able to confirm this impression.

A front line trench at Hill 60, summer 1915.

It was my turn for night duty, and I had a very disturbed night. There was a simply terrific struggle going on on Hill 60 which went on all night and I have never heard such a din: we are told that people there, who have been through the whole campaign, say that it was the heaviest bombardment they have ever experienced. The Germans have spent the last 24 hours bringing up reinforcements and more guns and literally trying to blow our people off the hill; they have been employing hand grenades very freely and apparently continually rushed forward, discharged a shower of hand grenades and then returned to their trenches only a few yards back. This sort of thing, combined with a terrific bombardment went on all night, and as the Germans got a footing onto the left of the hill, the situation is serious. Our losses have been very heavy, and already it has been necessary to get the assistance of one battalion from V Corps – 2/Camerons. However, we are still holding on to the line, but I think only by the skin of our teeth.

The battle raged on the following day.

This tremendous bombardment still goes on on our left: amongst other things the Germans have got a 17 inch gun with which they are shelling Ypres. They have any amount of ammunition and are trying to make Hill 60 absolutely untenable. We of course, for the moment, have not got the guns to compete with them owing to a lot of our guns having been withdrawn for use elsewhere [this would have been to the area around Neuve Chapelle for use in the British offensive there in March and in May at Aubers Ridge and Festubert]. *The Germans are taking advantage of this naturally enough and probably think we are short of ammunition as well. I cannot help thinking we ought to make a diversion to try and relieve the pressure on these poor devils* [in fact this was being done] *on our left who are getting such a slating.*

Things did improve, as was noted on 22 April.

A fairly quiet night and as some of the heavy guns which had been sent south have been brought back, and as they were able to put in a good deal of work on Hill 60 during the night, our position there ought to be more secure. We hear that we are holding the crest all right and that the Germans are unable to get a view over it which is the great thing. There are, however, a few bombers on the broken ground on the northern side of the hill which are rather a nuisance.

German soldiers with gas masks, quite as primitive as the early British ones. TAYLOR LIBRARY

The reason perhaps for both the ferocity of the German counter-attacks and the lull in the fighting for the hill might be found to the north; the Second Battle of Ypres opened on 22 April with the first use of poison gas by the Germans against British troops. Johnston was vitriolic in his reaction.

> *The Germans are using some form of asphyxiating gas. They are devils, there is no doubt about it, they are not going to stick at anything, fair or foul, in order to win the War. The use of asphyxiating gas etc is prohibited by the Hague Convention, and the Germans signed their agreement to this Clause, yet she is deliberately using batteries of tubes which spray our lines with gas. We can but hope that the day of reckoning, when it does come, will be a very heavy one.*

1st Battalion Royal West Kents

1/RWK had moved into the trenches opposite Hill 60 at dawn on the 17th. An hour or so before the mines were to be fired the Germans opened up with their artillery which resulted in a duel between the guns of both sides, during which it seems that the Germans moved up some of their men into the forward positions on the hill from the support lines, which were being shelled. When the mines were fired, at short intervals, at 7.05 pm, the artillery barrage came down, and a minute later the men of C Company rushed the position in eight different groups. The regimental history comments that some of the supporting KOSB, whose job was to assist in consolidating the new line, decided to use 'their shovels and picks quite freely on the heads of the Bosche'. The attack was so effective that the battalion suffered only seven casualties, a number of these the result of the debris from the mines. A German prisoner (of the 105th Regiment) stated

The British mines exploded with tremendous effect and must have killed a great many men. It was just like an earthquake and my whole platoon must have been wiped out.

Sergeant M Stroud DCM (who won his decoration at Neuve Chapelle in October 1914), a member of C Company, said of the attack,

We met with practically no resistance when we got into the German trenches, the effect of the explosions having killed or stunned the occupants. We found a German officer partially buried and some men at once began to dig him out. He rewarded them, when released, by drawing his revolver and shooting one of them. Needless to say he met his just deserts.

The craters were very large, the biggest being fifty yards wide and forty feet deep. Defences had to be made in the dark, and the utterly devastated nature of the ground made this a difficult task. However, soon after midnight a parapet had been built and two communication trenches dug back to the old British line, all of this being done under increasingly accurate and heavy German artillery fire – indeed some fifty German batteries of all calibres were directing their fire onto the hill. The result was that the whole battalion began to take heavy casualties, those in support as well as those in the newly established position. Before the new day broke the battalion was relieved by the KOSB, though two platoons were still on the hill when the Germans launched a counter-attack. All of these men (including Lieutenant Poland, a platoon commander) were lost in the resultant fighting, and none of their bodies were recovered.

Two companies (D and A) were brought up to assist with the defence of the hill; the craters on the left had their forward lips consolidated, but in order to shoot at the Germans a man had to expose a large part of his body, and many fell victim to German snipers. The

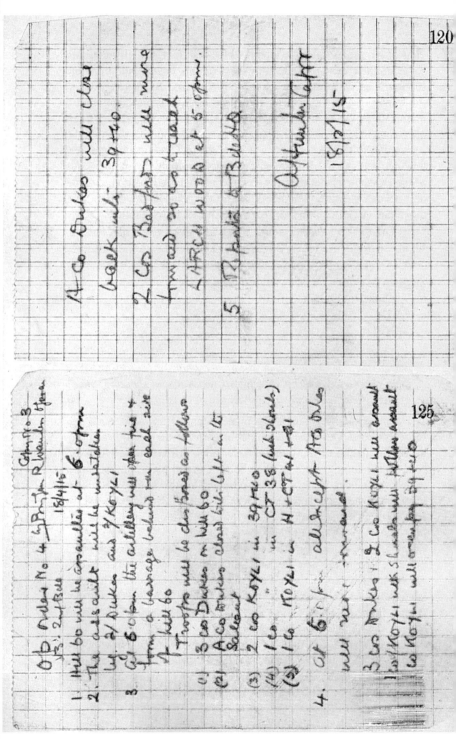

Copy of the original order for the attack on Hill 60, 18 April, 1915.

craters did help in an unlikely way, for many of the grenades and bombs which fell on the British lines rolled down into them and exploded at the bottom relatively harmlessly. At 8.30 am the battalion was relieved by 2/Duke of Wellington's.

In the course of the fighting some of the men had been affected by lachrymatory gas whilst washing; whether this was from canisters, waiting to be used for the German offensive a few days later, or from shelling is unclear, but if it were the former it would also explain why the Germans were keen to recapture the hill – they would not want canisters to be discovered, which would add credence to the report of a German deserter, on 14 April, to the French to the north that there was a gas attack planned within the next few days. Appropriate measures might then have been taken.

A German account quoted in the Official History of the problems that were faced with the loss of Hill 60 explains much:

> On the evening of the 17th April, Hill 60 in the sector of XV Corps was captured by the British after an explosion of mines. The fear expressed at the time that some of the gas cylinders dug in on Hill 60 had fallen into the hands of the enemy seems to have been groundless.

The battalion was to suffer one further misfortune: just as D Company was entering Ypres a shell landed in the middle of its remnants and caused several more casualties.[3]

2nd Battalion King's Own Scottish Borderers

B and C Company were to form the pioneer supports for the attack of 1/RWK; A and D were in support in Larch Wood. There was relatively little difficulty, apart from the problems of working in darkness amidst the great heaps of debris from the craters, in turning the German trench around and making it into a British fire trench; whilst the German communication trench was also blocked. However the real problem, as might have been anticipated, was on the right, nearer the railway line. These trenches were subject to enfilade fire from the Caterpillar and indeed this part of the line was never properly garrisoned. Thus B Company, on the left, were able to withdraw according to schedule, but C was still at their task on the right when, at 2.30 am, the Germans made greater efforts to remove the British. A, C and D companies now engaged in bloody hand to hand fighting, dealing with Germans who were able to crawl up unseen under the lee of the great lips created by the craters. Eventually 2/Duke of Wellington's relieved the battalion at 11.30 am, but not before they had suffered considerable losses. Amongst these was Captain Rupert

ZWARTELEEN HILL 60 TRENCH 38 RAILWAY BRIDG

Dering, the adjutant, who died of wounds shortly afterwards and is buried in Poperinge Old Military Cemetery, and Captain R Campbell who died of his wounds in London and is buried in Brompton Cemetery. An illustration of the difficulty of the position on the right is given by the killing of Lieutenant Hugh Malet, who was shot from behind in one of the craters near the railway – a clear indication of the variety of angles of fire available to the Germans. The KOSB left the hill, having suffered 10 officer casualties and 201 amongst the other ranks. They proceeded to the comparative shelter of Railway Dugouts, but it was not to be long before they saw Hill 60 again; whilst in the meantime they, and other members of 13 Brigade, were to go through some even fiercer fighting north of Ypres, to the east of the canal bank, as part of the desperate fighting to hold the line after the Germans had commenced their big attack.[4]

2nd Battalion Duke of Wellington's

The regimental account of the doings of this battalion are given as a report by Lieutenant CWG Ince, who was the adjutant at the time; this was first printed in the Times as *Eye-Witness at Headquarters in France* in April 1915.

> *At the time the mines were fired, the 2nd Battalion was in its billets in the town. Some of us were enjoying a well-earned and excellent dinner cooked by our soldier staff. It was not long, however, before we received orders to move up in support of the units of the 13th and 15th Brigades on Hill 60.*

Battalion HQ was in railway dugouts, along with two of the companies; one company (A) was in an old battery position in Zillebeke, and another company took up residence in dugouts in the railway embankment on the Bedford House side.

> *At 3 am on April 18th A Company was ordered up into the line and at 6 am the remainder of the battalion moved up in relief of 1/RWK and 2/KOSB, taking over the trenches these regiments had captured the previous evening. A Company were already in the advanced craters.*

QVR MACHINE GUN   THE CATERPILLAR   BATTLE WOOD

Poor old A Company in its advanced position suffered badly owing to the close proximity of the enemy. The latter, as already stated, had regained ground during the night prior to the Battalion taking over the hill. A Company was heavily bombed with hand grenades, and early in the day had severe casualties, which included its commander, Captain RC Milbank, who was badly wounded, subsequently dying of his wounds. [He is buried in Boulogne East cemetery.] *Things got hotter and hotter. Just before noon the Commanding Officer, together with his adjutant and a couple of orderlies, visited these advanced trenches. This was a most precarious journey, as the very shallow communication trench leading to them was almost blocked with dead and wounded. None of this small party were hit, however, either going or coming back, although at times in full view of the enemy.*

On his return, about noon, Lieutenant-Colonel Turner ordered B Company, augmented by one platoon from each of C and D Companies, to reinforce A Company, which for many hours had gallantly and grimly held its ground until nearly wiped out. It was whilst taking his men up to the craters that Captain Thomas Ellis was killed. [He is buried in Perth (China Wall) cemetery.]

About 4.30 pm an order was received from Brigade Headquarters that the battalion was to attack and dislodge the Germans from that portion of the Hill that they had regained during their counter-attacks made the previous night. Lieutenant-Colonel Turner at once issued orders for the remainder of the Battalion (ie C and D Companies less one platoon each) to move up into the craters in readiness, whilst 2/KOYLI occupied the trenches they vacated in readiness, and joined in to support the attack as second wave.

B Company was given the right section of the attack, C the centre and D the left section, whilst A Company, which had suffered so heavily during the day, was held in reserve. Battalion

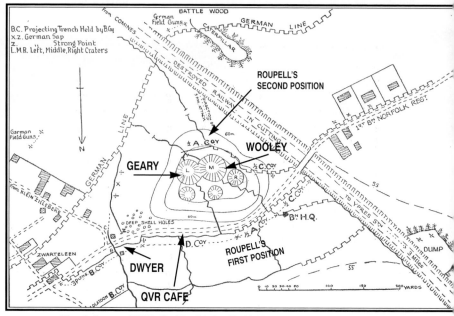

The defence of Hill 60, 19 - 21 April, 1915.

Headquarters was in the centre crater.

Under supporting artillery fire, with bayonets fixed, at 6 pm the Battalion went over the top. B Company reached their objective without much difficulty. C Company had to charge over some fifty yards of open ground and suffered very heavily, Captain Barton and a few men only reaching their objective. They, however, captured the trenches allotted to them, killing and capturing a number of the enemy.

D Company had some distance to charge over open ground and lost all their officers at the start, four being killed and two wounded. Ably supported by 2/KOYLI this company nevertheless captured the German trenches allotted as its objective. Not one inch of ground was lost.

Dusk was now rapidly approaching, and under cover of darkness, the trenches won were consolidated, the German communication trenches blocked and new communication trenches to our reserve dug.

It was whilst superintending the attack, accompanied by the adjutant [ie the writer of this account], *that Lieutenant-Colonel Turner was unluckily hit first in the right leg and a quarter of an hour later in the other leg, thus becoming a casualty.*

Beyond some unsuccessful grenade throwing, sniping and heavy shelling, no counter-attack was made that night by the

Germans on the captured trenches.

The attack and defence of Hill 60, a mere episode in the British operations, and a very minor occurrence on the whole of the front held by the allies, will nevertheless go down in history as amongst the finest exploits performed by British troops during the war. Officers who experienced the bombardment prior to the attack of the Prussian Guard on November 11th, and also underwent that directed on Hill 60 state, indeed, that the latter was by far the worse of the two.

What our troops withstood can to some degree be realised if it be remembered that the space fought over on the four and a half days between April 17th and 21st was only 250 yards in length, about 200 in depth. On to that small area the enemy for hours on end hurled tons of metal and high explosive, and at times the hill-top was wreathed in poisonous fumes. And yet our gallant infantry did not give way. They stood firm under a fire which swept away whole sections at a time, filled the trenches with dead bodies, and so cumbered the approaches to the front line that reinforcements could not reach it without having to climb over the prostrate forms of their former comrades.

In these circumstances the losses have naturally been very heavy. Nevertheless, they have not depressed the men, who are all, including the wounded, extremely cheerful, for they know that the fight for Hill 60 has cost the Germans far more than it has us.

The battalion had suffered fifteen officer casualties (of whom seven died) and 406 other ranks, of whom 29 were killed and 43 were missing, believed killed.

At this stage 13 Brigade was replaced by 15, with the addition of 1/East Surrey. This battalion was to win, over the next forty eight hours, three Victoria Crosses.

1/East Surrey

The regimental history gives a very full account of the extraordinary events during the time that 1/East Surrey was on the hill, and precedes it with a powerful account of the defences.

See Map
page 30

Three craters now lay approximately in a straight line close to the southern crest line of the hill and are shown on the map as (L)eft, (M)iddle and (R)ight. The left and middle crater formed a figure of eight, as their lips intersected at a point where their junction was below ground. The middle crater was slightly larger than the left, which had a diameter of thirty yards and a depth of twenty feet. The right, smaller, crater was separated by a few yards from the middle one. Two other craters lay to the rear, that is, near the northern crest line of the hill.

The defences at this time consisted of, roughly, two lines of trenches both of which started from a point near the railway bridge. The forward line of trenches ran from the bridge up the slope of the pimple towards the right crater, where a gap existed, beyond which the old German support trenches were held as the British front line and extended as far as the front of the left crater. Into these trenches opened two old German communication trenches which crossed No Man's Land from the German front line, one of which continued through the left extremity of the British front line past the left crater into the middle one, while a branch from it ran direct to the left crater. Both the old German communication trenches were blocked in No Man's Land at some distance from the British front line, and both branches of the continuation of the left hand trench were blocked again between the advanced line and the craters.

The left of the British advanced line was thus completely in the air, and the danger to this flank was increased by the existence of the German sap XZ. When the Battalion took over the position, C Company under the command of Captain AH Huth, who was to be subsequently killed, took over the whole advanced position from the bridge to the left crater.

The immediate support line of trenches ran along the line of the road from the bridge to Zwarteleen. A Company, under Lieutenant Roupell, took up position in the right trenches as far as the communication trench running up to the left crater, with D Company on his left and beyond them B Company, which had three platoons in the front line and one in reserve. At the base of the pimple, opposite the junction of B and D companies, the ground was pitted with large shell holes; and a little further to the left was the German strong point, Z, distant only twenty yards from B Company's right. Further again to the left and at right angles to the general front was the short trench BC, also held by B Company, with two ruined houses alongside it, which obscured the view into the shell hole area.

The machine gun section had five machine guns, four of which were with B and D companies covering the eastern slopes of the hill, and one was with C Company, near the bridge. 1/Bedfords were in support, based in the trenches and dug outs in and around Larch Wood.

The 19th April was, for most of the day, relatively quiet, although there was continuous German shelling of the position, although most of this fire was directed to the support trenches to the rear of the hill. At 5 pm there was a full scale bombardment of all the trench positions for half an hour or so, but the Germans made no move to launch an attack.

At 10 pm half of A Company, under Lieutenant Roupell, relieved two platoons of C Company which occupied the foremost part of the position, in the old German support lines; both companies had two platoons in the front and two platoons in the immediate support lines. Captain Huth was killed as he directed the extension of the line from the railway line to the right crater.

The early morning of the 20th was uneventful in the advanced positions, but the Germans maintained an accurate and harassing fire on the trench at the base of the hill, Germans were to be seen working on their sap at X, and an attempt was made to discourage them by throwing bombs from C, at the end of the short, projecting trench. This attempt failed, and the Germans determined to destroy the British block at that point by the use of their advanced field guns; a number of brave men managed to restore the block, which was essential if the men in this position were to be saved from lethal fire.

The Germans had also been working hard at Z, making it into a strongpoint overnight and equipping it with steel loopholes.

Situated as it was only twenty yards from the British trench, B Company suffered severely from its bombers and snipers. Every time one of the East Surrey men looked over the parapets near the strong point a German bullet went into or near his head, and in one place five men in succession were killed in this way while an attempt was being made to bring rifle fire to bear on the German working party at X.

A heavy barrage was brought to bear at about 11 am on the whole of the British position, obliterating much of the work done on the trenches, whilst many men were killed or buried by the explosions. The CO of the battalion, Major WH Paterson, along with his adjutant, Captain D Wynyard, moved along to D Company trenches to see what was going on. Captain Wynyard was killed by a shell whilst helping with some of the wounded; he and those killed with him were immediately buried behind the parados – but their bodies were subsequently lost and so they are commemorated on the Menin Gate. The lack of traverses and the destruction of the few that there were meant that the German shrapnel fire from their forward field guns was causing a large number of casualties on the right of B Company and the left of D Company.

Captain PC Wynter, commanding B Company, went forward at 2.30 pm to reconnoitre the A Company positions on the forward slope of the hill, to take them over at dusk. There he was wounded and taken for safety to a dugout, but this was destroyed by a shell and he was killed. He is buried in Railway Dugouts cemetery. To the left things were becoming tense once more; at 3 pm the Germans attempted to move men from Z in to the shell hole area to the right of B Company's position. They did this with the aid of snipers in the strong point, who effectively kept the heads of the British down. Private Edward Dwyer decided that the only way to deal with this situation was to jump onto the parapet and throw bombs into the German strong point, thereby allowing the defenders to man their parapet and fight off the attackers, assisted by cross fire from D Company on their right.

Private Edward Dwyer

At this time one of the strange quirks of war brought two brothers together; Lieutenant OI Nares commanded the left platoon of B Company, brought up at about this time; to his left was a company of 1/Cheshire, of 15 Brigade, commanded by his brother, Captain EP Nares.

The full blooded attempt by the Germans began at about 4 pm. Artillery of all calibres rained down on the position, including field batteries near the Caterpillar on the right and Zwarteleen on the left; A Company, in its exposed position, suffered in particular from the gunfire from the Caterpillar, with the shells pitching into the trench.

The bursting of shells was incessant and the noise was deafening. The little hill was covered with flame, smoke and dust, and it was impossible to see more than ten yards in any direction. Many casualties resulted, and the battered trenches became so choked with dead, wounded, debris and mud as to be well nigh impassable. Every telephone line was cut and all communications ceased, internal as well as with sector headquarters and the artillery, so that the support offered by the British guns was necessarily less effective.

One of the chief elements of the Battalion to suffer was headquarters; their dugout was destroyed, killing and wounding all but two men, and Major Paterson was dead. When the men finally left the position they carried his body out with them, and he was buried in the grounds of the Convent in Ypres; in due course he was moved to Bedford House, Enclosure Number 2. He also received the most unusual honour of being posthumously promoted to Temporary Lieutenant-Colonel.

In the advanced line the two platoons of A Company hung grimly on; the right trench, which bent back to join C Company's position, had been badly raked by fire and all but a handful of men had been killed. Lieutenant Roupell ordered a reserve platoon to come forward to reinforce the position and these men had literally to cut their way through the right hand platoon's position, the occupants of which had all been buried by the explosions which had devastated the trench. They suffered badly from the German fire, but managed to reopen communications with the left forward platoon, which had been in great danger of being completely cut off.

Lieutenant Roupell

Whilst this tremendous bombardment was going on the Germans had evacuated their own forward positions so that they would not become casualties of their own fire; after 5 pm the artillery switched their attention from the southern and eastern slopes and concentrated on the British positions to the rear of the hill and their communication trenches to the rear.

Germans began to push against the right of the position, emerging from the railway cutting near the Caterpillar and advanced across open ground towards the right crater. They were halted by British artillery (the observer had his position in the Dump), by fire from 1/Norfolks on the far side of the cutting, and the machine gun in C Company's position. This gun was operated by Corporal FW Adams who

> *was at the time single-handed, as during the bombardment both his gunners had been killed, while he himself was severely wounded. He continued nevertheless to fight this gun, though a portion of his jaw had been shot away, for more than half an hour until, soon after the German infantry attack was dispersed, he was killed by a solitary bullet through the head. For his heroism his name was subsequently submitted by the Battalion for the award of the Victoria Cross.*

Unfortunately he was not to receive it, and no other decorations were awarded posthumously.

Whilst C Company was fending off the Germans, A Company came under attack from German bombers who crawled up the old communication trenches. In support of them were a number of infantry who tried to push forward across the open in a series of short rushes. The defenders' trench was so narrow that they could not use the long handled bombs with which they were equipped; instead they threw the Germans' bombs back at them whilst others picked off the German infantry.

The Germans attack against B and D Companies was aimed at cutting off A Company by capturing the communication trench from D Company to the left crater and that crater itself. In fact this communication trench was occupied by a platoon of D, and these men were able to provide cross fire as the Germans, exiting from XZ sap, pushed into the deep shell hole area. This was a difficult position, not least because the strong point at Z had been equipped with two machine guns, which could bring heavy fire to bear on various parts of the British position from unlikely angles.

By this stage 1/Bedfords had moved up from their support position; it was becoming clear that the left crater was the main objective of the Germans, it being in such an exposed and vulnerable position and difficult of access by reinforcements. Lieutenant Roupell called for assistance and men of 1/Bedfords occupied the left crater; meanwhile Second Lieutenant Geary of C Company also heard the call for help and moved his platoon forward. He could not get there under cover, as the communication trench on the right was battered beyond practical use, and instead made for a gap through the debris into the left crater, where he and his men were greeted with a loud cheer from the Bedfords.

The Germans continued to pile fire into the position, causing casualties both to the men there and the reinforcements. Amongst those killed in the fighting was Second Lieutenant T E Norton, who had commanded the platoon which had held the communication trench to the left crater in the earlier German attack. He was shot through the head whilst firing over the lip of the crater. His body was lost, but found subsequently, which perhaps explains the fact that he is buried some miles from Hill 60, at Oostaverne Wood Cemetery.

Meanwhile the men of A Company in the advanced position continued to hold on, fending off attack after attack which invariably consisted of a fusillade of grenades followed by a charge of infantry; each time these were met by effective fire from survivors from the maelstrom of fire that had hit their position. Lieutenant Roupell, in overall command of this advanced position, was able to make use of darkness to get back to the sector headquarters to explain the gravity of his situation. Whilst there he had his eight wounds dressed, and then returned to take command of the position.

About 8 pm the German bombers managed to creep along their left communication trench into the extreme left of A Company's position. Because the trench had no traverses, it was possible to fire along it and keep them at bay, but they were also able to keep the British from reoccupying it by constant bombing; the left hand of the position became a No Man's Land of its own. Other Germans slipped into the prolongations of their communication trench which led into the middle and left crater. From the trench leading to the middle crater some

Lieutenant Roupell's wounds being dressed during the German counter-attack at Hill 60

commenced firing into the backs of the defenders of the left crater, whilst others followed the branch trench that led into the left crater. These were shot down at close range as they emerged and this attempt was eventually abandoned, the Germans falling back to the junction of the communication trench with the left of the advanced position.

Second Lieutenant Geary, having repelled this attack, was keen to know what was happening on his flanks, in D Company's and the advanced line. He sent three messengers to D Company but got no reply (for the simple reason that no messenger actually got to him), whilst he himself made his way across the summit to the advanced line. There he found that the situation was under control and that the hill would not be abandoned unless it was certain that there was no support behind them. On returning to his position he found that support was indeed available in the shape of the QVRs.

Second Lieutenant Geary,

Action was taken to recover the situation caused by the bombardment. The telephone wires between the companies were repaired and Second Lieutenant Geary oversaw the construction of a new trench on the summit of the hill which commanded the middle crater. A German flare showed up the Germans in the extreme left of

Second Lieutenant Geary hurrying under heavy shell-fire to a trench on the right of Hill 60 to get in touch with an officer.

the advanced trench, and from a point close to the new trench fire was brought to bear on them and another position established which enabled the British to fire along the old communication trench which had been the German route in the first place to the advanced line. The Germans were left crowded together and with little cover, and were therefore forced back, but continued to harass the British in the advanced line with their bombs from their original position in the communication trench.

The forcing of the Germans from the left of the advanced line led to a general easing of the situation, although fire continued to be poured into the left crater. Whilst Second Lieutenant Geary was going back for further reinforcements, just before dawn, he was badly wounded which was ultimately to lead to the loss of his left eye.

At dawn on 21 April the men were roused to prepare for a new attack; it did not come (at least for them) and at 6 am they were relieved by 1/Devons. The cost had been heavy : six officers were left out of the twenty one that started the action. The losses to the Battalion since their arrival in France had been very heavy – for example of the seven officers who were killed, four were attached from other battalions of the regiment; of the seven wounded, three were from other battalions or regiments. 106 other ranks were killed and 158 wounded.[6]

The three VCs of 1/East Surrey were awarded, for some unclear reason, over a surprisingly long period of time – the first (Dwyer's) in late May 1915 and the last (Geary's) in mid October 1915. Private Edward Dwyer was gazetted for his Victoria Cross on 22 May 1915.

For most conspicuous bravery and devotion to duty at Hill 60, on the 20th of April 1915. When his trench was heavily attacked by German grenade throwers, he climbed on to the parapet, and although subjected to a hail of bombs at close quarters, succeeded in dispersing the enemy by the effective use of his hand grenades. Private Dwyer displayed great gallantry earlier in this day in leaving his trench, under heavy shell fire, to bandage his wounded comrades.

He joined the army in 1912 at the age of sixteen, lying about his age: he had had enough of being a greengrocer's assistant. He was made use of for a while to bolster the war effort; as I write this I am listening to a recording he made describing the early months of the war. Dwyer was a devout Roman Catholic and married a nurse who had cared for him in France at St Thomas' Church in Fulham in December 1915. He was the youngest winner of the VC of the war up to that time, being just 19. On 4 September 1916 he was killed just outside Guillemont on the Somme, and he is buried at Flat Iron Copse cemetery, situated in a particularly beautiful site on the old Somme battlefield. Lieutenant George Roupell's VC was gazetted on 23 June 1915.

Private Edward Dwyer, singlehanded, disperses a German assaulting party and saves a trench.

For most conspicuous bravery and devotion to duty on the 20th April 1915, when he was commanding a company of his battalion on Hill 60, which was subjected to a most severe bombardment throughout the day. Though wounded in several places, he remained at his post and led his company in repelling a strong German assault. During a lull in the bombardment he had his wounds hurriedly dressed, and then insisted on returning to his trench, which was again being subjected to a heavy bombardment. Towards evening, his company being dangerously weakened, he went back to the battalion headquarters, represented the situation to his commanding officer, and brought up reinforcements, passing backwards and forwards over ground swept by heavy fire. With these reinforcements he held his position throughout the night, and until his battalion was relieved the next morning.

He returned to France as adjutant, then was promoted G3 (an operations staff appointment) in XVII Corps, before going to Third Army in the same appointment in September 1916. In December 1916 he was made Brigade Major (a job of great responsibility, and much sought after) in 105 Brigade.

After the war he was part of the British force that went to assist the White Russians in the civil war there, and was captured by the Red Army; he was repatriated in 1920. He remained in the army and had a very varied career with postings in Canada and China, which was followed by an adventurous time in the Second World War. He narrowly evaded capture after the brigade which he commanded (36) disintegrated under a German onslaught, spent two years in hiding in a farm in France, returned to Britain via Spain and then commanded (by some strange coincidence) 105 Brigade. He became President of the Old Contemptibles Association in 1973 and died the following year, just short of his 82nd birthday, at his home near Shalford, itself only a short distance from Guildford, the county town of Surrey.

Second Lieutenant Benjamin Geary was gazetted for his VC on 15 October 1915.

> *For most conspicuous bravery and determination on Hill 60, near Ypres, on 20 and 21 April 1915, when he held the left crater with his platoon, some men of the Bedfordshire Regiment and a few reinforcements which came up during the evening and night. The crater was first exposed to a very heavy artillery fire which broke down the defences, and afterwards, during the night, to repeated bomb attacks, which filled it with dead and wounded. Each attack was, however, repulsed, mainly owing to the splendid personal gallantry and example of Second Lieutenant Geary. At one time he used a rifle with great effect, at another threw hand grenades, and exposed himself with entire disregard to danger in order to see by the light of the flares where the enemy were coming on. In the intervals between the attacks he spent his whole time arranging for the ammunition supply and for reinforcements. He was severely wounded just before daylight on 21 April.*

Geary was the son of a clergyman, and it seems likely that he might have been thinking of the Church early on, as he went to Keble College, Oxford, a High Anglican establishment founded in the nineteenth century. Almost immediately after the war, having just about recovered from another serious wound on the Somme in August 1918, he became a clergyman. He served for a while in the army as a chaplain but emigrated to Canada in 1928 but worked with many military organisations for the rest of his life. He died in 1976, just short of his 85th birthday.

Queen Victoria's Rifles (9th London Regiment)

This Territorial battalion was amongst the earliest to arrive in France, in November 1914, and was attached to 13 Brigade. In the fighting on Hill 60 it was to win the first Territorial VC of the War. In the original attack it took little part, although one of the battalion's machine guns was situated on the far side of the railway bridge and provided valuable covering fire both for the British attack itself and against subsequent German counter-attacks. The events on the hill on 20 – 21 April 1915 as far as the QVR were concerned may best be described, for the most parts, by their winner of the Victoria Cross, Lieutenant G Harold Wooley.

At dusk [on 20 April] *we were ordered to go up to Larch Wood and went by way of Zillebeke Lake and village. There we met a barrage of tear shells and 5.9s and a good deal of random rifle fire, so going was difficult, but we had remarkably few casualties. Sergeant M Brawn kept my men amused by explaining to them that the show was well worth a shilling a day. When we arrived at the wood we found A and D companies had been sent up to the front with stores. They got mixed up in the counter-attacks and made some progress, probably occupying the German support line. Information came back that they were short of SAA* [small arms ammunition], *so Captain Cowtan was ordered to take up Nos 7 and 8 platoons (Wooley and Houghton) with a fresh supply. We started about 10 pm, but it was about midnight before we had struggled up the communication trench which was blocked with wounded stretcher bearer parties, messengers etc. The communication trench was narrow and very much knocked about. As I was leading a man, I think it was a runner of C Company, just in front of me, was hit by a bullet in the thigh. He couldn't walk, and as the trench was too narrow to allow us to pass I tried to bind him up on the spot. He saw it was difficult and would keep the SAA party waiting, so he asked us to leave him at the bottom of the trench and walk over him as they needed the*

Major Thomas Prior Lees, killed at Hill 60.

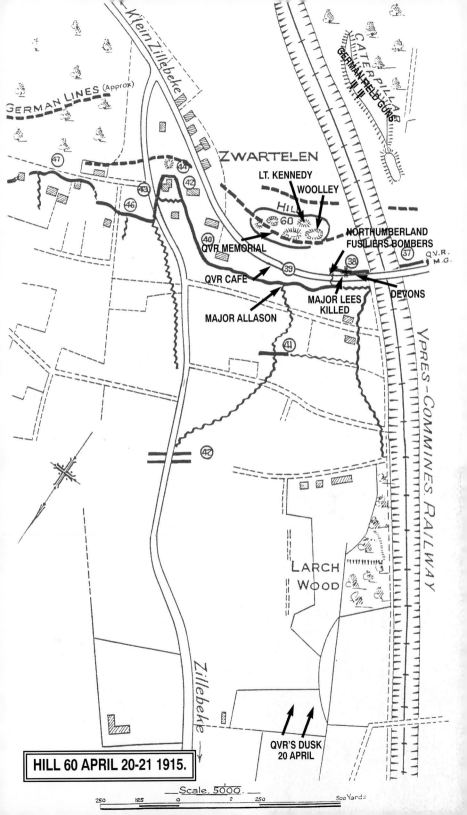

HILL 60 APRIL 20-21 1915.

Scale, 5000.

Larch Wood

Zillebeke

Kleim Zillebeke

GERMAN LINES (Approx)

ZWARTELEN

CATERPILLAR
GERMAN FIELD GUNS

YPRES-COMMINES RAILWAY

LT. KENNEDY
WOOLLEY
HILL 60
QVR MEMORIAL
NORTHUMBERLAND
FUSILIERS BOMBERS
QVR.
M.G.
QVR CAFE
DEVONS
MAJOR LEES
KILLED
MAJOR ALLASON
QVR'S DUSK
20 APRIL

250   125   0   250   500 Yards

ammunition very badly on the hill! We managed to get him moved to a wide spot and he was properly bandaged up there. I heard afterwards that he was all right.

My orders were to report to Major Lees and bring back a written report on the situation, so that if necessary Nos 7 and 8 platoons should stay up to help hold the front line. At the junction of the communication trench and Trench 39 Major Allason of the Bedfords, who was detonating bombs, directed me up to the hill and I took on the leading men with a few boxes of SAA and soon found Major Lees. There was a comparative lull except for rifle fire. Major Lees [who was commanding the QVR on the hill] said he could not tell what the situation was himself and asked me to go around the hill with him. The craters were full of men in support. Just in front of them we met Westby and Summerhays; both were very cheerful and went over the ground with us. In the dark it was very difficult to tell much about the position, but Major Lees was quite satisfied that he had plenty of men to hold on with, and in fact thought it would be better to withdraw some by day as they were too crowded in the craters.

I started back with this message and promptly got lost in a network of derelict trenches, shell holes and barbed wire. I had just put myself right and picked up a party of four men, also lost, when a heavy barrage was let down on to our old front line about fifteen yards

Second Lieutenant G H Woolley encouraging and directing a handful of men during the terrible fighting on Hill 60.

in front of me. I had to lie doggo for some time and then went on and found Major Allason, who told me that Nos 7 and 8 platoon might return, so I passed down word and they began to file back. Just at that moment a messenger came down to say that the German counter-attack had driven our men back, so Major Allason ordered me to call back the two platoons to go and help. I passed the message down, but apparently Major Allason stopped the men going up with me until he had more detailed information, for when I arrived on the hill and reported to Major Lees I found only three men with me. However there were plenty of men in the craters.

Major Lees went off to the right towards Trench 38 to try and reorganise the men. I remained in the right crater and began bombing with Hales grenades. Almost at once a message came that Major Lees was killed. The bombs quickly ran out and someone found a box of jam-pot bombs. I had no matches to light the fuses and borrowed a box from Summerhays, who just then came into the crater. Soon after he was killed, but I did not see him. The jam-pot bombs were not a success, but at intervals more Hales were sent up by Major Allason and most of them I sent on to an officer of the Bedfords (Lieutenant Kennedy) in the left [ie the middle] crater – he worked there for a long time throwing bombs, standing in a very exposed position in his shirt sleeves. The sergeant who was helping me was killed, and soon afterwards a bomb exploded on my head but only tore the cap [at this time the British had not been issued with steel helmets]. One of our MGs was sent up and took up a position in the left crater – he worked extremely well, which encouraged us a lot as the German MGs were very active, but before long it was knocked out.

Hall was sent up to ask how things were going and I told him we should hold the craters all right, but soon afterwards the Germans started shelling us with field guns they had brought up to the Caterpillar, about 300 yards away on the other side of the cutting. These just tore away the lip of the crater, causing very many casualties, and also caught the wounded lying at the back of the crater, who tried to go down the communication trench, or rather the track, to Trench 39. I started to go to the other crater to consult with Kennedy about asking for more men, and on the way met another officer of the Bedfords wounded badly in the arm. Just as I reached Kennedy the German field gun switched on to that crater and the first shell broke his knee. Assisted by one of his own men I got him bandaged up, and our own stretcher-bearers, who were doing splendid work, carried him back.

I was now alone with both craters and the ground to the right to look after, so went from one group to another – they were huddled up in little groups where the crater lip or parapet was not blown away – cheering them up and keeping them firing. Ammunition was getting short and rifles jamming, so we had to collect rifles and SAA, plenty of which was lying about the craters. I had just left the left crater when two shells knocked out most of the remaining men; the wounded struggled for the communication trench at the back and the rest tried to back with them. Luckily I was standing so as to bar the way and the men in the right crater beckoned to them to come back as well. So I examined each one and sent the unwounded and slightly wounded back, and they manned the left crater again. That was our most trying moment. Fortunately the guns on the Caterpillar ceased fire shortly afterwards; probably several of their shells fell short and the Germans could not help killing their own men. Their fire was most discouraging, for we scarcely heard a round fired from our own batteries all the while. About this time a message came up from Battalion HQ to tell me that all QVR men were to go back to Larch Wood, but that would have meant deserting the crater as there were only a few Regulars, Bedfords and East Surreys, on the left, so I said we would wait for a relief.

Soon after a young officer of the Devons arrived from Trench 41 in the left crater and reported to me that he had three of his platoon left, but that they were cut off as the parapet on either side of them was blown away and three MGs were raking the parapet above them. I told him to get them to crawl along into the left crater which was very thinly held. There were now just two small groups of men in the left crater, one in the right and another in the gap towards 38. The Devons' officer told me that his battalion was coming up to relieve us, which was good news, as the men were very badly shaken. I had previously sent back word asking for reinforcements, but without result. Probably the messengers were too excited to deliver the message. I did not like to send more messengers, as they did not return, so I arranged with the Devons' officer to go back myself and report the state of things to Major Allason. He told me that a relief was coming at once and the news bucked up the men a lot.

But the relief never came. So after a while I again went and told Major Allason that I did not think that the men in the craters would last much longer. I found two officers of the Devons with him and their men in the communication trench all waiting. Naturally their progress had been very slow and difficult and they had about 80 casualties coming along the railway. I arranged to take up 30 men to hold the craters by day, and led the captain up, the men following. When we reached the crater I found only the captain with me, and his sergeant major came along with a message that the men had been sent back to the trench on the right. I at once went to see what was wrong. They had been called off to 38 trench, as a platoon there waiting for relief saw the party coming and sent a guide to bring the relief to themselves. I explained to them that their relief was coming in time and took my party back. Meanwhile in the communication trench to 38, blocking the whole trench, I found 60 trained bombers of the Northumberland Fusiliers! They

Photograph taken at the end of the war. Note that he is wearing red tabs and the cap badge of a staff officer. He was gazetted for the MC in 1919.

had been specially sent up to the hill, but their officer had been killed and they were misdirected. In consequence they were waiting for some hours in the communication trench – trained bombers, with a plentiful supply of bombs -when we had been urgently needing them. I ordered their Sergeant to take fifteen of them to help the Devons in the craters and sent the rest back to support. It then only remained to see the Devons properly established and bring off the QVR men who were left – about fourteen of them altogether.

Riflemen Sidney Seymour gave his description of what happened on the hill to a local newspaper.

It was while my company were in the trench just at the rear of the first line that things started. We had only rifles and bandoliers, but nevertheless had to 'get on with it'; we went up to the front right into the thick of things. It was an awful sight. The trench filled with dead and wounded, bullets pouring across, shells bursting, grenades and trench mortars hailing in. How anyone came out of that place alive is truly remarkable. The magnificent way our boys held the ground was a sight to see. A mere handful of 'rabbit shooters' keeping back the German hordes. I myself was knocked about by a shell which burst near me, but fortunately nothing was broken. I lost the use of my left arm and side for about eight hours and was badly shaken. So unfortunately I did not see the thing through. It was a bad day for us as the company at roll call numbered 26 men and one officer. Corporal Peabody did fine work in attending the wounded. I had an awful shock the next morning as he did not turn up for some hours after we were relieved. When he did turn up he broke down just as we had all done. The strain was awful and to see your pals go one by one adds to the horror. We cried like children and were completely broken up.

The total of fatal QVR casualties was surprisingly small – two officers killed, one missing (later known to have been killed), 15 other ranks killed and 107 wounded. This was partly because not half the battalion were involved in the battle, partly because numbers on the hill were kept to the minimum required to defend the position – more men

QVR (9/London) Memorial on Hill 60 in the 1920s. Note the chaotic state of the ground with a network of trenches and numerous dugouts.

TAYLOR LI

would merely have become easier targets for the random nature of the German hand grenade attack. Major Lees was buried near the Larch Wood dugouts, but his body was lost in later fighting along with that of the other officers who were killed, and their names are to be found on the Menin Gate. Wooley's VC was gazetted on 22 May 1915.

For most conspicuous bravery on Hill 60 during the night of 20 – 21 April 1915. Although the only officer on the hill at the time, and with very few men, he successfully resisted all attacks on his trench and continued throwing bombs and encouraging his men until relieved. His trench during all this time was being heavily shelled and bombed, and was subjected to heavy machine gun fire by the enemy.

He was training to be a clergyman at the outbreak of the war, and took up the ministry after it, followed by a job at Rugby and then many years as Chaplain at Harrow. For the rest of the war he held a number of staff jobs, after taking some time to recover from the stress of the action at Hill 60 and the subsequent German gas attack a few days later. It was during the battle for Hill 60 on 7 May that that the adjutant of the QVR, Captain George Culme-Seymour, was killed, a momentous event for Wooley, who married his widow in June 1918.

Wooley dedicated the QVR memorial on Hill 60 and retained his military connections. During the Second World War he served as an army chaplain in Algiers; his own son, Rollo, a spitfire pilot, was killed in action in 1942. He became Vice Chairman of the VC and GC Association and died at the age of 76 in 1968.

The British had held the hill, but the new onslaught by the Germans that followed, and the first use of poison gas against British troops, was to result in its loss for over two years.

1. *Military Operations France and Belgium 1915,* compiled by Brigadier-General JE Edmonds and Captain GC Wynne. Macmillan and Co, 1927
2. MSS: *My Diary at the War*, Alexander C Johnston
3. *'Invicta'With the 1st Battalion The Queen's Own Royal West Kent Regiment in the Great War,* Major CV Molony. Nisbet and Co, London 1923
4. *The KOSB in the Great War*, Captain Stair Gillon. Thomas Nelson and Sons nd
5. *History of the Duke of Wellington's Regiment [1st and 2nd Battalions]*, Brigadier-General CD Bruce. Medici Society 1927
6. *History of the East Surrey Regiment* Vol II, Col HW Pearse DSO and Brigadier-General HS Sloman CMG DSO. Medici Society 1923
7. *The History and Records of the Queen Victoria's Rifles 1792-1922*, Major CA Cuthbert Keeson VD. Constable and Company 1923

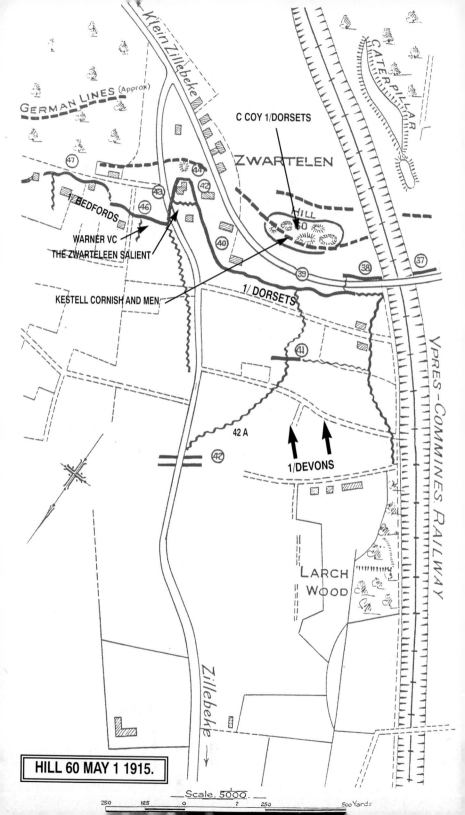

KleinZillebeke

CATERPILLAR

GERMAN LINES (Approx)

C COY 1/DORSETS

ZWARTELEN

47

44

43   42

HILL
60

1/BEDFORDS   46

WARNER VC

THE ZWARTELEEN SALIENT

40

39   38   37

1/DORSETS

KESTELL CORNISH AND MEN

41

42 A

42

1/DEVONS

LARCH
WOOD

Zillebeke

YPRES - COMMINES RAILWAY

HILL 60 MAY 1 1915.

Scale, 5000.

250   125   0   2   250   500 Yards

Chapter Two

THE FIGHTING OF MAY 1915: THE GERMANS RECAPTURE HILL 60

Hill 60 was to have an important place in the history of many regiments in the British Army, but on 1 May 1915 its significance lay in the fact that here, for the first time, a gas attack failed.

On this day the hill was held by 1/Dorsets of 15 Brigade, having relieved 1/Devons at 3 pm the preceding day. The men had, by this stage, been issued with an utterly rudimentary respirator, consisting of flannel and gauze, with instructions to wet them in case of attack; in anticipation of an attack, the respirators were already tied around the neck.

At 7.17 pm the Germans opened fire with a heavy bombardment on the hill and, before the sentries could raise the alarm, clouds of yellow and white gas were shot out of nozzles from the far side of the cutting, to take advantage of the south easterly breeze. The gas was directed at trenches 38, 40, 43, 45 and 46 - that is to the immediate left and right of the hill. This was accompanied by rapid German fire along the line, which then shifted to the railway cutting. C Company held the crest of the hill, and were in real trouble. Major Cowie, commanding the battalion, reported after the battle,

> *No officers left, so I cannot say for certain what precautions had been taken. They suffered heavily, so the presumption is they were unprepared for gas.*

The German tactics were to isolate the Dorsets both from reinforcements from the rear and from support from the flanks. The situation was saved largely by the prompt action of Lieutenant Kestell-Cornish and his platoon. The lieutenant seized a rifle and jumped onto the parapet; urged his men to do the same and then opened fire into the cloud. In fact he and his men were not badly effected by the gas, probably because they were standing well above ground, and thus away from its concentration: the gas was heavier than air and was at its strongest in the narrow confines of the trenches. In fact only four of his

View of Hill 60 from the British trenches.

platoon were able to stand with him, but their rate of fire convinced the Germans that the gas had been of only limited effect.

Kestell-Cornish survived this attack, went on to win two MCs, but died of wounds in June 1918 whilst serving as a captain on the divisional staff, and is buried in Boulogne East cemetery.

Meanwhile, in support, men of the Dorsets, 1/Devons and 1/Bedfords (the latter on the left) were hurried into the line, with Captain Batten of B Company taking over control of the situation on the Dorsets front. In due course Major Cowie moved up to the hill and took over; he then moved over to the left, to a part of the line called the salient, which was then garrisoned by the Devons and

> *found the deep and narrow trenches blocked with dead, with many others dying in terrible agony. It was a deplorable sight and one which no eyewitness can ever forget.*

By 10 pm the situation had returned to a state of tense calmness (!). The Dorsets history gives a review of the casualties.

> *An examination of the casualty returns brought to light the terrible ravages caused by the gas. They showed Second Lieutenant Butcher* [buried in Reninghelst Churchyard] *and fifty two other ranks dead; and in addition six officers* [of whom Second Lieutenant Roberts died, buried in Bailleul Communal Cemetery] *and two hundred other ranks were admitted to the field ambulance. In addition thirty two other ranks were missing, men who had crawled away to die, and whose bodies were*

A machine-gun section wearing the first gas masks, Ypres 1915.

located afterwards. Only one man was killed and one wounded by shell or rifle fire.

Second Lieutenant Cornish was sent to hospital two days later, suffering from the effects of gas, but was able to return to duty in a week's time, having flatly refused to be sent to England in accordance with medical advice.

A subaltern in Captain Batten's company, B, wrote an anonymous article for the Dorset press.

At about 7 pm I came out of my dugout and saw a hose sticking out over the German parapet, which was just starting to spout a thick yellow cloud with a tinge of green in it. The cloud came out with a hiss that you could hear quite plainly. The gas did not come directly towards us but went slantwise, then our trenches being so close to the gas went into part of the German trenches as well as ours. They bolted from theirs when they got a whiff of the filthy stuff [an interesting point to note is that the Germans were never particularly good at making effective gas respirators], *a few of our men staggered away down the hill, some got into a wood behind it* [ie Larch Wood] *and died there, as the ground was low and the gas followed them, others only got as far as the mine head and communication trenches. The Company in support* [ie B] *on my left moved up into the firing line, as did also half of my platoon, consequently I was left with a few men to do all the rescue work. My men were splendid; they all came with me into the gas, except the ones I ordered to stay behind, and we must have saved scores of lives. The men in most cases were lying insensible in the bottom of the trenches, and quite a number were in the mine head, which was the worst possible place. The best place after the first rush of gas was in the firing line, being the highest point.*

I was the only officer not in the firing line, and I should think quite two hundred men passed through my hands, some died with me and some on their way down. The Battalion had, I believe, 337 casualties. I can't understand how it was I was not knocked out; it must have been the work I had to do. I was simply mad with rage, seeing strong men drop to the ground and die in this way. They were in agonies. I had to argue with many of them as to whether they were dead or not. Why we got it so hot was because of the closeness of our trenches to the Germans, and this affair does away with the idea that it is not deadly. I saw two men staggering over a field in our rear last night, and when I went

53

and looked for them this morning they were both dead. Altogether, I suppose, one hundred or two hundred men and two or three officers are dead or will die of the stuff. Am absolutely sickened. Clean killing is at least comprehensive, but this murder by slow agony absolutely knocks me. The whole civilian world ought to rise up and exterminate those swine across the hill.[1]

On the left of the Dorsets, 1/Bedfords had been holding the line for some time, having relieved 1/Cheshire on 25 April. Although the German gas attack was chiefly directed against the hill, the right of the Bedfords position was affected, and all the men there were violently sick, with 22 admitted to hospital subsequently, of whom two died. Because of the disastrous impact of the gas on the Dorsets, the trenches to the Bedfords right were deserted or, at least, defenceless. The actions of Private Edward Warner were to win him the VC - he was amongst those who moved into one of these deserted trenches, though already badly gassed, and where the gas was at its thickest. He held his portion of the trench and remained there until he collapsed, subsequently dying of its effects.[2] His VC was gazetted on 29 June 1915.

Private Edward Warner

For most conspicuous bravery near Hill 60 on 1 May 1915. After Trench No 46 had been vacated by our troops, consequent on a gas attack, Private Warner entered it single-handed, in order to prevent the enemy taking possession. reinforcements were sent to Private Warner, but could not reach him owing to the gas. He then came back and brought up more men, by which stage he was completely exhausted, but the trench was held until the enemy's attack ceased. This very gallant soldier died shortly afterwards from the effects of gas poisoning.

His body was lost in subsequent fighting, and so his name is to be found on the Menin Gate.

Alex Johnston noted the night's events on Hill 60 in his diary for 2 May

The Germans again used asphyxiating gases which I'm afraid knocked out a number of our men [of 10 and 12 Brigades]; they did the same thing in their attack last night on Hill 60, and in spite of using respirators, which we have just got and as a matter of fact are very poor ones, about fifty men have died already from the effects of the gas which causes a form of acute bronchitis.

Gas had been withstood for the first time, but the cost had been very heavy - 90 men killed by gas in the trenches or front line area; of the

207 brought to the nearest aid stations 46 died almost immediately and 12 after long suffering.

Hill 60 is lost.

The fighting in the Ypres Salient had been intense since the commencement of the German onslaught on 22 April. The Official History notes

> *The mound, even by the 21st April, has been described as a mere rubbish heap of shell and mine torn earth, timber and dead bodies, and the fighting of the ensuing days had churned up and pulverised this scene of desolation. The British trenches were shapeless cavities; there was no other kind of shelter, and the enemy was less than a hundred yards away.*

The line was held on the morning of 5 May by 15 Brigade - 1/Norfolk, 2/Duke of Wellington's and 1/Bedfords in the line; 1/Dorsets in reserve in Larch Wood dugouts and 1/Cheshire and 6/King's in dugouts on the south west of Zillebeke lake.

At 8.45 am the Germans released gas against part of the line held by 2/Duke of Wellington's. The men were dog tired after a restless night and particularly heavy fighting over the preceding three weeks, and most were asleep in their trenches with the exception of the sentries. Only one of these saw the gas coming, and he promptly gave the alarm.

See map on page 67

Standing Orders for a gas attack were that the men were to evacuate that part of the trench effected and move to the flanks, and let the supports charge. However, the gas came from the flank, and instead of spreading over a section of trench, it ran along the length of it. In addition, the gas was exceptionally thick, and the respirators proved practically useless. After some fifteen minutes of the gas flowing, the line was more or less abandoned and the Germans were able to take over all but a small part of the front line on the lower slopes of the hill.

The Dorsets rushed the left of the position and secured a communication trench leading to the hill and then remained locked in close combat for the rest of the day. At 11 am the Germans released more gas on the north east part of the defences, against the Bedfords; their right, in the Zwarteleen Salient, gave way, thereby increasing the gap, but the left held on until 1/Cheshire could be rushed up from their digging job in Hooge to help to plug the gap, assisted by a company of 6/King's. Gradually the Germans were forced back from the positions that they had captured, though the crest of the hill remained in German hands.

A counter attack by 13 Brigade - the brigade which had first captured the hill - was launched at about 10 pm. However this was broken up, not least by enfilade fire from the Caterpillar and Zwarteleen. As the Official History states,

> Hill 60, even if it could be captured, could not be held unless a wide extent of the enemy's front on either side of it was also secured.

A final, small scale, attempt was made at dawn on 7 May which failed dismally. The hill was to remain in German hands until June 1917. The fighting at Hill 60 had cost the 5th Division over 100 officers and 3,000 other ranks. It almost certainly cost the Germans similar, or greater, numbers to get it back.

2/Duke of Wellington's

After the battering the battalion suffered at the time of the capture of Hill 60 it had had some time to recover; included in this process was the arrival of drafts of some 350 other ranks and 15 officers by 24 April; on 1 May several more officers joined, and a draft of 230 arrived on 2 May. In the intervening time the battalion had also been involved, though usually only in support or in reserve, against the German attack

ZWARTELEE

to the north of Ypres.

On 4 May 2/Duke of Wellington's relieved the Devons in trenches 38, 39, 40, 42, 43 and 45, completing this operation by 3.30 am on the 5th. The gas had a devastating effect as the regimental history reports:

See also map on page 124

> *before anything could be done, all those occupying the front line over which it swept were completely overcome, the majority dying at their posts, true heroes. By this foul means the Germans quickly got possession of trenches 40, 43 and 45, there being practically no one left to hold them. Captain GW Robins, East Yorks attached, was the last man to leave of the few who managed to crawl away, and he, poor fellow, died in agony that night from the effects of the gas.* [He is buried in Railway Dugouts cemetery.]

2/Duke of Wellington's did manage to hang on to the support trenches in the right rear, 38 and 39 and joined with the Dorsets in their counter attack. At the end of the day the only officers left were the Commanding Officer, Captain Barton, and his adjutant; the Transport Officer, the Medical Officer and the Quartermaster - all the other fifteen officers were casualties of whom 10 were killed, died of their wounds or were missing. The battalion was reduced to 150 other ranks.

HILL 60

1/Dorsets

The Dorsets started the day extremely badly, with the fatal wounding by shell fragment of their CO, Major Cowie, at 5.45 am. He died some days later in England. Captain Ransome, the new commanding officer, described what happened.

At 9 am a message, 'Gas coming over,' was telephoned from the front line, and simultaneously a considerable number of troops could be seen retiring along the railway line. C and D Companies, very weak after their numerous gas casualties on the 1st, were ordered forward at once to support 2/Duke of Wellington's. As a stream of gassed and demoralised men continued to pour down the railway line, A and B companies were ordered forward ten minutes later. By this time all the telephone lines both to the front and rear had been cut by the enemy bombardment, and the gas was very thick, even at Battalion Headquarters.

When at length the telephone line to 38 trench had been repaired, information came in that showed the situation to be: the Germans were holding Hill 60, portions of 39 and 40 trenches and the Zwarteleen salient. 2/Duke of Wellington's had

been badly gassed, and the Dorsets were holding 38 and the greater part of 39 trenches.

There seemed to be nothing, either in the shape of troops or trenches, to prevent the enemy from pressing on into Ypres itself. And at about 11 am it seemed as if this appreciation of the situation would prove correct, for parties of the Germans had begun to infiltrate towards Zillebeke. To meet this menacing situation, the details of Battalion Headquarters, supplemented by men partly gassed, were placed to cover the gap in positions from which they could bring fire to bear towards the north. To add to the gravity of the situation, repeated messages came in from the front line to say that our shells were falling short.

The arrival of 1/Cheshire calmed the situation somewhat; when the battalion came out of the line it was reduced to 173 all ranks, whereas it had gone in to the line 800 strong. Yet in the actual fighting only one officer and 14 other ranks were killed; there were vastly greater numbers of wounded and gassed. When the battalion returned to the Hill 60 sector on 20 May it had been restored to full strength, numbering 1100 all ranks. There it suffered from steady attrition in the new situation, with the Germans holding Hill 60, the Zwarteleen

TRENCH 39

Salient and the greater part of Trench 40, though the Dorsets were able to eject them from part of that during their later tour in the sector, on 23 May.

1/Cheshire

The Cheshires were rushed up from Ypres to help stem the flow. Almost as soon as they arrived their CO, Lieutenant-Colonel A de C Scott, was killed. He is buried in Zillebeke Churchyard

Second Lieutenant Arthur Greg provides the details of what happened to part of this battalion in their regimental history. It is a quite extraordinary story of a period of time in the trenches, and is quite graphic in all its detail; this more than justifies the amount of space which it is given in this book. His account is preceded by a description of Ypres in the immediate aftermath of the opening of the German offensive.

Two of us thought it would be rather interesting to go and look at the shops. We knew that we were the first body of men to visit Ypres after the precipitate retreat of the majority of its inhabitants. The town was, however, never entirely deserted. We went into various houses where chimneys were showing signs of

TRENCH 38

A street scene in Ypres.

life, and in most we found several aged Belgians with long beards and curious little peaked caps. They were generally sitting in a more or less dazed condition in front of their stoves. The windows were generally smashed, and often the doors. But they preferred to stay in their old homes rather than flee into the unknown.

News of the attack reached the battalion just as it was returning to its

RAILWAY BRIDGE
AND CUTTING

billets in the ramparts in Ypres.

We only had a few minutes to get ready. We had no time to divide the rations which we had drawn in bulk the night before. We were to go up light, so we left our coats and heavy things in the casemate. B Company had to go first with ten minute intervals between each platoon; my platoon was the first to go.

It was broad daylight. There was a tremendous cannonade in progress. What we were all asking was how far the Germans had pushed through. When we finally emerged on to the bridge [that is across the moat by the Lille Gate], after crossing that hellish three hundred yards, we wondered what was in store for us. We all carried our little cotton wool mouth pads around our necks ready for instant use.

As soon as we were well in the open we extended and proceeded, expecting any moment to be fired on by some concealed Germans. We passed almost under the very guns of our field batteries. They were pounding away at high pressure and seemed almost as excited as we were. It was rather a comfort to get past that spot as the Germans were answering their fire with considerable vigour.

The Lille Gate, Ypres, 20 September 1917. In dugouts beside the gate were, at one time the headquarters of the 1st Australian Division.

After a good many halts, we finally came to the end of that shell-swept two miles of open country. It was piping hot and we were terribly thirsty. The sights we saw on the way up were not calculated to cheer us much. We passed many groups of men dead or dying, some wounded and all badly gassed. Most of them were writhing in awful agony. The colour of their faces and the noises that they made turned our blood cold. We could do

THE CATERPILLAR

nothing for them. We had to push on, leaving them gasping for breath and dying under that pitiless sun. We reported ourselves to the adjutant of the remains of the regiment in support. [This was the adjutant of the Dorsets.] *We were told that we must go up to the fire trench and work with the regiment there. Our first business was to clear the fire trenches and communication trenches of all the corpses. My men worked till they nearly dropped. Water was scarce. We tried the puddles at the edge of the railway line. The water was filthy and brown, but it was refreshing. Sometimes we were fired on at close range from somewhere behind. The Germans had broken through and were still breaking through. Nobody quite knew where the next English troops on our left were.*

At one time we noticed a large number of men dashing down the hill about 70 yards on our left. We thought they were the remains of the regiment holding the hill, so we held our fire. It was hard to see amidst the clouds of dust and bursting shells. It was not long before we realised that they were Germans. The artillery of both sides were frightfully at a loss. We were shelled by our own guns. The Germans were shelled by theirs. On the skyline, the crest of the hill, which must have been about 80 yards away, we watched sand bags appearing; we saw shovels wielded by unseen hands hammering them down. Our picked marksmen fired and tried to hinder their work of consolidation as much as possible.

After a few hours I was told by my new CO that I was to go as far along the trench to my left as possible. We started. Suddenly out of one of the communication trenches one of C Company officers appeared alone. He seemed quite cheerful, but very tired. He had been doing a little investigation on his own and informed me that if I kept along my present path I should be into the Germans in another forty yards. We pushed on, however. I was in front of the platoon.

The trench had been badly shattered and was lined with that curious yellow colour that spells lyddite.[3] The trench was full of fresh German dead piled over each other. A lucky shell of ours had done its work and slaughtered about 20 Germans. We crawled over these. They were very wobbly, and the going was bad. On turning round a traverse a bullet hit the sand bag just beside my face. I looked up and saw a dirty unshaven German staring at me with a rifle in his hand. He was shooting over a

64

The horror that could be caused to man and defences by shell fire.

barricade. The range was about ten yards. I withdrew and took cover behind a corpse. There were many Mauser rifles lying about and plenty of ammunition. I loaded and peeped over the corpse. We both fired simultaneously and bobbed down again. It was a weird sort of duel. Neither of us cared much about it. Then, from my prostrate position, I started making a little barricade of my own. My friend behind the barricade had several more shots and so had I, but although hideously close, they did not take effect. This duel must end. It wasn't good enough. I think we both realised this about the same time, as my adversary did not expose himself any more when I was looking. Meanwhile, my platoon had all come up and were waiting. I passed the word for sandbags to be filled and passed up. In this way I was able to build a sort of barricade. I then withdrew a few yards and piled up what bodies I could with the help of two of my men against the barricade. We had to keep very low as shots came from behind, from the flank and from the front. It was an unhealthy spot, and I didn't like the carpet of Bavarian bodies; their limbs were so horribly arranged and their shoulders didn't make a firm footing. After leaving some good men near the barricade, I managed to plunge along past men and corpses to the healthier end of the platoon, bearing rather a grudge against my new company commander [of the Dorsets].

The first thing was to settle down a bit and see that the men

65

had proper fire positions, and that there was sufficient ammunition. The next thing to do was to find some hand grenades. My sergeant found a box of the jam-tin variety with which I thought I might get my own back on the bearded Hun who mounted guard over the barricade.

On one of the German dead I was lucky enough to find a water bottle full of the most excellent ice cold coffee. What nectar that drink seemed. I didn't stop to think what mouth had last drunk out of that neat little aluminium bottle. It was at this period that I made the biggest blunder of any. I hurled two bombs in quick succession over the barricade. There seemed to be some confusion behind those sandbags in front of me and my men were vastly pleased. It was not long, however, before we got a full dose of those horrid little black grenades that the Germans fling so accurately. For the next half hour or so we had a great duel. Many of my men were unfortunately hit. One can only hope that our jam tins did some damage on the corresponding side. An officer of the Dorsetshire Regiment had his head blown off just as he was handing me a new box of grenades. I felt very upset as I felt that somehow I was to blame for having urgently demanded more grenades.

After an hour or so there was an inevitable lull. Both sides were getting tired. By this time it was growing dusk. No one was looking forward to the night. Those Germans were horribly close and greatly outnumbered us. Besides, nobody knew how many of the enemy there were behind, and what possibilities there were of us being surrounded. I had sent various orderlies to report on our position. Most of them, I learnt afterwards, had been hit on the way. We were told to hold on where we were if possible. We were then having rather heavy cross fire from the German machine guns. They seemed to know exactly where their men ended and ours began.

As it grew dark there was an ominous lull in the firing that had been so continuous during all day. We expected that a large number of Huns might at any time leap over the barricade and engage us in a hand-to-hand fight. Possibly they might hold us on the left, or barricade side, whilst another party might come up the communication trench in the rear and attack our other flank. By that time I had only about twenty men in the trench, except for one or two more or less useless men who had been partially gassed earlier on in the day. One or two men were sent

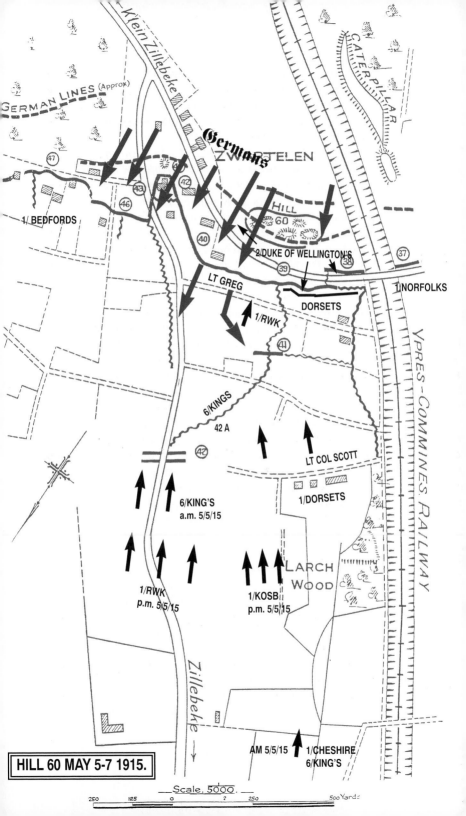

GERMAN LINES (Approx)

KleinZillebeke

47

43

42

46

40

39

37

38

Germans
ZWARTELEN

Hill
60

CATERPILLAR

1/BEDFORDS

2/DUKE OF WELLINGTON'S

1/NORFOLKS

LT GREG

DORSETS

1/RWK

44

6/KINGS

42 A

47

LT COL SCOTT

6/KING'S
a.m. 5/5/15

1/DORSETS

1/RWK
p.m. 5/5/15

LARCH
WOOD

1/KOSB
p.m. 5/5/15

Zillebeke

YPRES — COMMINES RAILWAY

AM 5/5/15

1/CHESHIRE
6/KING'S

HILL 60 MAY 5-7 1915.

Scale, 5000.

250   125   0   2   250   500 Yards

as sentries down the communication trench that ran direct to the rear from the right of my platoon.

About 8.30 pm the whole hill was brilliantly lit up by thousands of star shells that were all starting from one point, and this sort of Crystal Palace show was accompanied by a most extraordinary crackle. Seldom have I seen such fireworks. Our rifle fire or shell fire must have set light to a large store of German star shells. The effect was wonderful and weirdly strange, considering the surroundings. During the whole of that memorable night there were not many moments of complete darkness. About 9 pm our artillery started with renewed vigour. They were pounding the German trenches on our front and our left front. The HE was well mixed with shrapnel that added its glaring flashes to the other various lights of the night. There was going to be a counter-attack; we wondered what the regiment would be and where they would be starting from. We were not left long in doubt. Soon a tall captain in the KOSB appeared, closely followed by what afterwards appeared to be two companies. [These were men from 2/KOSB] *He told me they were to attack the trenches in front of us and were going to start from my trench at 10 pm.*

At the allotted time they climbed over the parapet. The order was to go half right. They were met with a storm of rifle and machine gun fire from the hill. Our artillery had not yet stopped and soon theirs started. The poor Scots were simply blown back with lead. They started again and went half left. Their wounded were pouring into my trenches. The sounds were terrible, men shrieking, the fierce cackle of machine gun fire and the cruel shriek of the shrapnel. This was battle. When the next volley of star lights went up there were noticeably more bodies in No Man's Land. Wounded and belated Jocks were still returning, some helping other wounded back or bringing in the body of some comrade. These shattered remains of a fine regiment all found their way back to my already overcrowded trench and its continuation to the right.

After about half an hour the rifle fire to our rear seemed if anything to increase. After a bit, on looking round, we saw a straggling line of dim figures with bright bayonets looming out of the darkness, and coming towards us. Who could they be? [Almost certainly they were 1/RWK] *When they were nearly on us we noticed the English service caps. I heard an English*

68

officer shout, 'Now boys, in at 'em.' And they were soon in on us. We worked miracles for the next second or two to make ourselves recognised as friends. It still puzzles me why there was not more damage done.

This was a new mass of overstrained and intensely excited men to cater for. My trench was an absolute inferno. More wounded poured in and most of our field dressings had been given to the Jocks. The uppermost thought in my mind was what a horrible mess to disentangle in all this fearsome noise. The Germans on our left meanwhile were vastly amused. We heard them laughing and shouting. I was quite afraid of an attack at that moment as we could not have put up much of a fight. I had been able to discover no Jock officers and the only officer of the last regiment to arrive was a rather bewildered Second Lieutenant who had only been up at the front for three days. We divided out the line between us and prepared for the worst, it was not a bright outlook.

Shortly after this, my companion received word that he was to withdraw what remained of his detachment. Then I learnt that the Dorsetshire Regiment had retired to rest and that the Jocks had to hold their line. That thinned us out a bit and soon we were more or less comfortable again. It was an anxious night and everybody prayed for dawn as they had never prayed before. In daylight we could at least see what was coming, and there is something very comfortable about daylight after the strange artificial light of the night.

We all felt rather bedraggled the next morning and as we had had nothing to eat for over 24 hours, we began to search for food. It's extraordinary what food there is to be found in an average trench, if one only looks for it. Our search revealed some stale bread, and a good many tins of bully beef. This we shared and felt a slight alleviation of our hunger. I then crept into a dugout down the communication trench for a few minutes snooze, but was soon aroused by a Jock captain who wanted to speak to me. He told me amongst other interesting things that Brigade HQ wanted to know if I could blow up the barricade with gun-cotton. I told him I would see if it were possible.

I crept over our own barricade keeping very close to the front parapet. On looking for a second round the corner of a sandbag, I saw for a moment a German head and rifle at a loop hole. They had loopholed their barricade and had made it almost impossible to approach. I withdrew my head and just escaped a bullet. I then rolled back over the barricade with incredible speed and sent a report to the Brigade stating what I had seen and how, in my opinion, it was impossible to destroy the obstruction with gun-cotton.

In comparison to the previous night that morning passed almost uneventfully. My trusty servant at one o'clock came and announced that dinner was served. He was a merry fellow and I went to see what he had produced. He had cut and buttered me some almost clean bread and had opened a tin of beef. It promised to be a good meal, but towards the end, the smell of the corpses was so great that I determined to see if we could not remove them. I was standing on one grey-jacketed fellow and superintending the removal of another when I was conscious of a terrific blow. I went down like a log and was next aware of a loose, horrid and disconnected feeling about the lower part of my face. I was bleeding like a fountain, and my mouth seemed full of obstacles. I tried to spit them out and found they were teeth. I remember distinctly some fellow saying in an agonised whisper, 'He's had his false teeth knocked out.' This annoyed me horribly, as I had always been rather proud of my teeth. My servant then more kind-heartedly than wisely poured the remainder of his water bottle into my mouth. The water, it afterwards transpired, had been drawn from the moat round Ypres, this at best was nothing more than the town sewer, and as shells had been falling in it like hail for a fortnight, the purity of the water that I received in my wound could not have been very great.

My servant then applied all the bandages and field dressings that he could find. I watched his horrified face with interest and noticed that everybody that saw me looked strangely at me. I then stumbled down the trench. I heard the shout everywhere, 'make way, it's an officer.' I was at the time in my shirt sleeves with no hat and covered in blood. Some of the Jocks recognised me and said, 'It's that Cheshire officer that's got hit.' I heard everything. I noticed everything, especially the looks on people's faces.

It was not long before I arrived in a very shaky condition at a big dugout that was serving as a dressing station. [This was in Larch Wood.] *The roof was low and I had to kneel. Even the doctor looked horrified when he took off the bandages, and quickly bandaged me up again, giving me some morphia. I sat against the wall of the dugout and found that the man lying at my feet had been hit in the arm and kicked me violently in his writhings.*

At last they injected me with more morphine and I began to feel easier and happy.

At one time I thought I should not live as I was bleeding so furiously. I thought it a pity that one more so young should have to go. I then thought that if I did recover I should be so disfigured that no lady would ever look at me again, and this depressed me horribly. I remember writing my fears on a piece of paper and showing them to the CO, who came to see me. He smiled and was very kind.

I was then asked if I could walk and said I thought I could. Two of the company stretcher bearers helped me along. I had one arm round each of their necks. My servant brought up the rear with my pack and odd things. We had the best part of a mile and a half to cover along the railway line, which was still being shelled. I did not mind that now a bit. I was not for stopping now once I had started. I had to have a good many halts on the way. One of the stretcher bearers, an old friend of mine, kept consoling me that I was safe on the way to Blighty, and it would be a long time before I ever saw Belgium again. He meant well, but I was not duly impressed with his arguments.

When the farm was finally reached [Transport Farm] *I had to lie on some straw for two hours before an ambulance came. It was then getting dark. The journey in that shaking ambulance was too awful and seemed interminable. At last the car slowed down and finally stopped.*

After lying out on a stretcher in the garden, waiting my turn to be examined, they took me into a crowded room, placed me on a table, and redressed me and gave me an anti-tetanus injection.

I was then returned to the stretcher in the garden.

My faithful servant was as solicitous and tender as any nurse but he could not do much. I lay out there for most of the night, but was at last put into another ambulance, which was more of a torture than the first, as my face was growing stiff.

It was not till next morning, Friday, May 7th, that I reached Bailleul and a bed.[4]

Arthur Greg was typical of his generation of subalterns; he was the son of a Major-General and was educated at Rugby and New College,

Dressing station: note the salvage of equipment in the top right rear.

Oxford, joining the army when he was nineteen. At the outbreak of war he was a member of the OTC and had been sent to the Front in September 1914, serving with the Sherwood Foresters. He was invalided home at Christmas 1914, though he returned to the front early in January 1915, this time to 1/Cheshire. After his severe wound received at Hill 60 he spent some time recovering before rejoining his battalion, being promoted captain in November 1915. He became battalion bombing officer and in September 1916 left to join the RFC. He returned to France to serve with 55 Squadron in April 1917, but not for long. On 23 April he set off with seven other D.H.4s to bomb the German ammunition depot at Boué. Of the six who carried out their mission of dropping two 112-lb bombs each, his plane was the single victim of the seven single-seater fighters that attacked them. He is buried at Jussy Communal Cemetery, some twelve kilometres east of Ham.

See map page 64 Whilst 1/Cheshire had been desperately trying to hold the line, they were supported by 6/King's, whose men advanced towards Hill 60 in an approach which ran from northern side of the Zillebeke to Klein Zillebeke road (Knoll Road) to the far side of the railway. Much of their work was involved in securing the communication trench 42A, which ran from Knoll Road in to Trench 39, this position being held throughout the night of 5 May by men of C Company. In fact the Germans had managed, at one point, to get into part of 42 A and, making use of the shallow valley and the cover provided by high, flowering weeds, get to within easy viewing distance of Larch Wood;

72

it was men from this group that were responsible for the killing of Lieutenant-Colonel Scott of 1/Cheshire. By late evening, however, this particular threat had been removed.

The return of 13 Infantry Brigade.

Although 13 Infantry Brigade had been fighting on the hill only some two weeks earlier, the fighting in the interval to stem the German advance that had commenced on 22 April resulted in further very heavy casualties - thus for 2/KOSB another 260 odd had to be added to the 220 or so that the assault on Hill 60 had cost.

Thus many of the men who were rushed to the Hill 60 front on the afternoon of 5 May were new to the sector. The battalion moved up to Larch Wood with orders to launch an assault at 10 pm. One of the new officers was Captain Mayne (actually an officer from the HLI attached to the KOSB). C and D were to front the assault, with A and B in support and to consolidate the gains. The attack was to be launched from the trenches opposite the hill, with 1/RWK attacking on the left. A twenty minute bombardment merely warned the enemy of the imminent attack. C's charge was crushed almost immediately (as described by Greg above), whilst D managed to make progress on the right, but came under highly effective enfilade fire from the Caterpillar and were ultimately bombed out of their gains. Four officers were killed and eight wounded, whilst there were 130 OR casualties.

The problem for both the KOSB and 1/RWK was that the extent of the German gains was unclear, especially on the left, that is to the north of the hill. Sergeant Robinson, of 1/RWK, described the scene:

> *The night was extremely dark and the ground was much encumbered with old wire, and also cut up by old trenches and shell holes. What with the darkness, the difficult ground and the general obscurity of the situation, the attack never developed properly.*
>
> *This is an instant of the sort of thing that occurred. One platoon was directed along a road which, though plainly marked on the map, had been quite obliterated on the ground by heavy shell fire. Having nothing to guide it, this platoon got too far to its right and, when it reached trenches supposed to be held by the enemy, found them occupied by British troops.* [This was almost certainly Greg's position, see above.]

In fact Sergeant Robinson was, at the time of this attack, the only one in the unit who had seen the ground before in daylight. This gives some indication of just how badly mauled members of 13 Infantry Brigade

Captain George Culme-Seymour.

had been in the fighting since 17 April. This unsuccessful attack cost the battalion another 110 casualties.

On 7 May a further attempt was made on the hill by, amongst others, 2/KOYLI, with the QVR in support in Larch Wood - the latter battalion now numbering only some 320 men. In fact, and as things turned out, the battalion was not more than peripherally involved in this further doomed attack on Hill 60, but their adjutant, Captain George Culme-Seymour, was killed whilst liaising in the front line trenches (39 and 40) with the Cheshires and trying to establish exactly what the situation was.

> *We buried him, under severe fire, just north of and near the boundary of Larch Wood. Major Dickins read the burial service over the body and Captain Roe, the MO, and four sergeants, among whom were McMoran of the gun team and myself [Sergeant Crossthwaite], as representatives of the regiment, lowered him into his last home. I don't think there was a man of us who did not break down, so great was our love for and admiration of the gallant soldier who had so much to do with the making of the battalion. It was an irreparable loss.*

It was his widow that Wooley married in due course.

Although there were numerous other attempts to dislodge the Germans from the hill, and there were various minor alterations in the line, the position around Hill 60 was to change little until the momentous events of June 1917. The British counter-attacks had failed because of a lack of artillery and manpower - more especially fresh infantry - and because of their heavy commitments elsewhere in the nerve-wracking days of late April and May 1915.

Much of the interest of the fighting in Hill 60 now moves underground.

---

1. *History of the Dorsetshire Regiment 1914 - 1919,* anon. Henry Ling Ltd. 1932
2. *The Story of the Bedfordshire and Hertfordshire Regiment,* the Regimental History Committee. nd
3. Lyddite was a high explosive, composed chiefly of picric acid, and used in making explosive shells. It got its name from Lydd in Kent, which was for many years one of the principal homes of the Royal Garrison Artillery. The German defence of their use of chlorine gas was that the British had beaten them to it with Lyddite, whose fumes, they argued, were just as deadly as anything they were using.
4. *The History of the Cheshire Regiment in the Great War 1914-1918,* Arthur Crookenden. nd
5. *'Invicta'* op cit
6. *Queen Victoria's Rifles* op cit

Chapter Three

MINING AND THE BRITISH ATTACK OF
7 JUNE 1917

Much of the action at Hill 60 took place under ground culminating, most famously, in the sprung British mines of April 1915 and June 1917. Thanks to the interest and generosity of Colonel Phillip Robinson, late RE, I have obtained an unpublished manuscript by the Assistant Inspector of Mines at GHQ, Major HR Dixon, MC, and the first part of this chapter is based on a chapter from that book in which he gives a basic introduction to the mysteries of military mining. Comments in brackets are mine.

'A mine gallery was what an Irishman once described as nothing at all, being merely a hole. The size of the gallery varied according to the conditions, but was usually about four feet by three feet in section, though wherever possible it was made rather higher to give greater comfort in walking along it. Except in hard chalk (such as at Vimy Ridge), it was timbered with mine casings of 2″ or 3″ planks fitted together.

The methods of work differed from those in use in civil life, because it was very necessary to avoid giving any hint to the enemy listening in his own tunnels for sounds of our working. Therefore the essential atmosphere of mine galleries was their silence (an atmosphere perhaps more familiar to readers as akin to an instruction for 'silent running' in a submarine). In clay it was a question of scooping out the ground in front with special tools, and Sir John Norton-Griffiths was the first to introduce his system of 'clay-kicking' in the early days of 1915 in the Ypres Salient. Men, lying on the floor of the gallery, with their backs partially supported by a plank wedged across it, would push their scoops into the face with their feet. In this way really silent working was possible, and screws were used instead of nails for fastening timbers.

The clay or earth was filled into sandbags and hoisted up the shaft or incline to the surface, where it was dumped at night, wherever possible in a site secure from the observation of enemy aeroplanes. A visible accumulation of bags would always give the game away to the enemy and bring retaliation in the shape of heavy shelling of the shaft head or counter-offensive by the enemy miners. Men and officers worked in their socks as often as not, and the quietest whisper was the only form of speech allowed.

The laying of a charge was a considerable undertaking in the case of a large mine. We were fortunate in the choice of the principal explosive used. Ammonal was an Ammonium Nitrate explosive containing some 18% of TNT and about an equal quantity of powdered aluminium. The effect of the aluminium was to so raise the temperature of the gases caused by the explosion that the lifting effect was enormously increased, while the shattering effect of the Ammonium Nitrate and the TNT was not reduced. It was therefore particularly suitable for blowing large surface mines, while its crushing effect on any enemy galleries within a given radius could be relied upon.

Also it was a powder which was convenient for packing into petrol tins or sandbags, and would not be exploded if struck by a bullet, but only if fired by a proper detonator.

If a charge was to be left in position for a long time it was always laid in petrol tins to protect it from the damp. Otherwise it would be put into sandbags, double ones, in a dry gallery. (In fact the charges I have seen in situ in recent months in old mines were contained either in boxes, or in rubberised sandbag type containers, secured at the mouth with two pieces of wood, tarred and bolted.) The electric detonators were often protected further by being placed in small rubber bags, rubbered and taped until thoroughly water tight. All tins were sealed with pitch in the case of a wet mine. It will be understood how carefully these details were carried out when it it is remembered that some of the Messines mines were actually under water for more than a year, and yet not one of them failed when the day came. (Famously, of course, one went up near Plugstreet Wood almost forty years after it was laid, induced, probably, by a lightning strike. Major Dixon explains why the mine was still there - for this see the footnote.[1])

Firing was usually done by a push-down exploder from a dugout in the support trench, but sometimes current was taken from the electric lighting plants of the 'Alphabet' Company (a specialist company that installed and maintained lighting, vent machines and the like). Successful explosion of the mine usually produced rum or whiskey from the appreciative infantry. On one occasion I had laid my valued watch beside the exploder, and missed it later on, and all my satisfaction was spoilt by the apparent theft. But a little while later the faithful Round (his orderly) produced it, having taken the precaution of pocketing it for me, and great was my relief.

Listening for the enemy was naturally one of the most important duties of a Tunneller. In chalk it was never possible to do the actual excavation in silence, and the sound of working could be heard a long way off. Special listening devices, of which the best was the French geophone, were of great help. This instrument was an adaptation of a donkey's long ears to the doctor's stethoscope. Two microphones placed on the floor of the gallery were connected by two rubber tubes to a headpiece fitting over the ears. These were moved about on the floor until to the listener the sound appeared to be coming from straight in front of him. It was then clear that it was coming from a direction at right angles to the line joining the two microphones. The compass bearing of the noise was noted and another bearing obtained from an adjacent gallery. The intersection of the two lines on the plan would indicate the position of the working enemy.

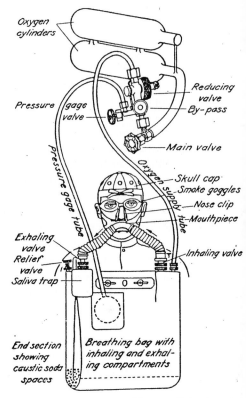

Fig. 4. Circulating System of Fleuss, or Proto, Apparatus.

Circulating System of Fleuss, or Proto, Apparatus.

Various tricks and devices were used by both sides to confuse their opponents. Dummy picks, operated by strings from a safe distance, were employed by the Germans, but their lack of imagination caused them to work these so regularly, and with such an even rhythm, that they were always detected. The main idea was to draw the opponent's attention away from the gallery where offensive work was really going on. When a charge was to be left in position for some time it was usual to leave an electronic microphone buried in the charge, the listener sitting back in the workings, out of all danger. At Hill 60, a few days before Messines, the electric listener in the charges indicated that the enemy was within a few feet of them. Very careful tests were made and it was decided that by zero hour he would be within three feet, and he was heard at this distance just prior to the blow. Accurate estimates of the German rate of working enabled us on this, and many other occasions, to predict his position by a given time.

It was all rather like a blindfold game of chess in three dimensions.

Once at Bully Craters I discovered that the enemy were very close to our gallery. We were then on the defensive on this front, and had laid a small charge at the end of the old French gallery discovered when we took over. There was fifty feet of solid sandbag tamping between me and the charge (the tamping ensured that the charge was not channelled back along the tunnel which led to the mine), but the enemy had apparently come across diagonally from a flank and seemed likely to break in to the open part of our gallery within less than 12 hours. Fissures in the chalk often led to slight miscalculation of distance, and it was quite possible that he was really nearer than this, so I at once sent word to Major Morgan at Company HQ, cleared everyone out of the gallery, and prepared for a long, lonely vigil in the dark. I had borrowed a revolver, but it never occurred to me until years later that a bomb or two would have been more than useful. About three hours later I heard footsteps coming along our own gallery. It proved to be a telegram with a message for me from home. The history of that telegram should warn all senders of non-vital messages in wartime. It had been sent by the Army post office to the Company billets, from which some poor tired fellow had been sent up the line to find me. He had two miles of communication trench to traverse before reaching my dugout, and a further mile under Private Round's guidance to get to the particular mine. Another man thereupon took off his boots and brought it down in the dark to me!

However no harm was done beyond that, and to my nerves, and a few hours later Major Morgan, having obtained permission from Division, sent word to me to blow the charge already laid, and we had no further trouble from that direction for some time.

Whenever a mine was blown by either side, one of the most important things was to ascertain at once the damage to our own galleries. All underground explosions give rise to heavy fumes, of which the most deadly constituent is Carbon Monoxide. This gas is the same weight as air and, having no smell, cannot be easily detected. Even 0.1% of this gas is dangerous after some minutes, and it was never safe to enter a gallery immediately after an explosion except when wearing oxygen apparatus.

On the wonderful War Memorial at Edinburgh may be seen figures of the miner's friends, the canary and the white mouse. Both of these creatures are much more sensitive to the action of the deadly gas than a human being, and it was necessary to have a supply available for testing purposes. At the RE stores at Calais a big aviary was maintained. The white mice occasionally presented the official mind

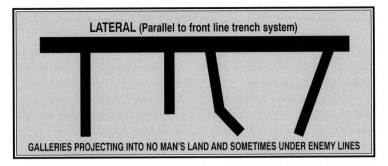

LATERAL (Parallel to front line trench system)

GALLERIES PROJECTING INTO NO MAN'S LAND AND SOMETIMES UNDER ENEMY LINES

with unusual problems. Most of the ingenuity of people making returns had to be spent in explaining deficiencies, and one officer, at least, was completely defeated by the white mice, for he had indented for six, and no doubt six were sent, but on arrival there were 27! There appeared to be nothing in King's Regulations or other authority to indicate the correct procedure for such an emergency.

The canaries were naturally great pets and were kept in cages outside our dugouts. There was an amusing incident one day when an infantry major 'won' our canary, and refused point blank to believe that he had stolen an article of RE Store. Reference to Brigade was finally necessary before we got it back.

One bird that perished for its country almost deserved its fate. I had put it into a small travelling cage for an inspection of a gallery, and it looked very pathetic, and aroused my sympathy. But as I watched it, the creature laid an egg and drew still more sympathy, which was however soon withdrawn, for it proceeded to make a hole in the egg and eat it. And the feeding of it had been my special care for weeks!

There is on record a story of another bird that caused the greatest alarm along an important front for some hours. A mining offensive was in progress of which we thought the enemy had no idea, when the canary escaped and fluttered out of the trench onto a picket in our wire. It was of the utmost importance that the bird should not be seen by the enemy, and with great reluctance orders were given that it was to be shot by a sniper. The bullet was almost bigger than the bird, and it is not to be wondered at that the sniper missed the mark. The canary was, however, sufficiently disturbed to flutter out into the middle of No Man's Land. A staff consultation was held at once, with the result that a well directed shot from a heavy trench mortar put an end to the anxiety.

By the middle of 1917 the science of mining defence had been brought to a high level, and the danger of listening work greatly reduced by the establishment of central stations, in connection with as

79

many as thirty projecting galleries driven from a main lateral gallery along the front.

The listener had a switchboard similar to a telephone board, and by plugging in to each gallery in turn could detect any enemy working in ample time for protective mines to be blown at the threatened point.

It has often been asked how it was that such a complete ascendancy was obtained over the enemy in underground warfare, and the true answer seems to be that their officers seldom descended their mines, and that much of their mining labour was derived from men sentenced to field punishment. On our side no disgruntled man was kept in a mine five minutes, as he might prove a danger to the safety of the rest. I have no idea of what the rank and file really thought of their officers, but the fact remains that they were prepared to follow them anywhere, and to undertake jobs at their request of the most arduous and dangerous nature, which is certainly a tribute to the men, and probably to the officers as well. Certainly the men were such as any man might be proud to lead. The vast majority were specially enlisted colliers from England, Scotland and South Wales, and no doubt North Wales too. Their military training, such as it was, had to be acquired in the front line.

One of the most interesting examples of mine fighting tactics, correctly applied, was at the Bluff, a point on the Messines salient about a mile south of Hill 60. It was the best place in the vicinity for observation purposes, and was therefore one of the first places in which mine warfare developed. A complicated series of shallow tunnels had been developed by both sides, many mines had been blown and the result was a jumble of small craters. But for a while here the enemy was slowly gaining the upper hand and it looked as though we might have to abandon our trenches at this point. It was accordingly decided to drive an incline deep under his defences and to cut off the enemy mine system altogether. The mines were so shallow in his system that careful listening from the surface by night patrols, combined with underground observation, had enabled the Australian Company in the line to fix the exact position of the portions nearest to us. In due course the deep mines were blown, and a party broke through from the surface in No Man's Land into the enemy workings. They took with them a telephone, paying out the wires as they went along. Owing to the various devices by which telephone conversations could be picked up, special codes were in common use in the front line. But in this instance the Australians, with their usual dislike of normal procedure, produced one of their own. The first message that came to the eager listener was, '240 feet Johnnie Walker.' This was probably equally as clear to any German waiter as to the recipient, for they were indeed 'going strong'. The whole enemy system was captured and added to our own and the Bluff was secure.

The scale of mining operations cannot better be indicated than by stating that by the middle of 1917 there were over a hundred miles of British mines and tunnels along the front; during the war the British fired over 3,000 mine charges. The average rate of progress was about three feet per eight hours, and work was continued on in continuous shifts. In subways (such as at Vimy Ridge) where silence was not demanded, a rate of up to eight feet per eight hours was often maintained for a gallery six feet by four feet in the clear.'

The Mines of 17 April 1915

This mining operation was the most ambitious yet undertaken by the British in conjunction with infantry operations. The work began using men recruited from the 1st and 3rd Battalions of the Monmouthshire Regiment who were attached to the 1st Northumbrian Field Company RE which worked under the direction of Major DM Griffiths, who was the assistant to the CRE (Commander Royal Engineers) of 28th Division. In due course these men were absorbed into 171st Tunnelling Company, and Major Griffiths returned home due to ill health after the battle died down towards the end of April.

Griffiths kept his mines very secret, but occasionally privileged officers were invited to accompany him personally. On one such occasion he took the commander of a neighbouring Field Company,

An artist's impression of a miner at work close to the front.

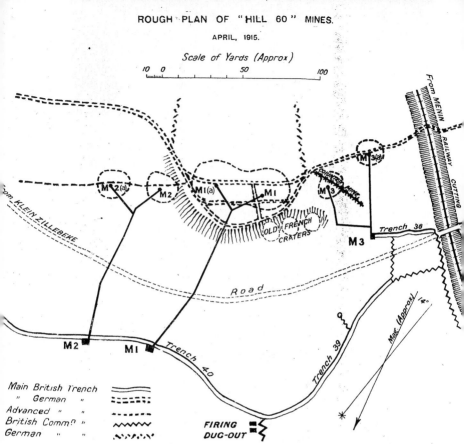

Scale of Yards (Approx)

Major JR White, and his adjutant; the expedition was something of an ordeal, as Griffiths was very deaf. The adjutant relates the story.

> *At one point he announced that we must all run for about eighty yards because of German snipers. He then shambled off to lead the way, with White and I following at suitable intervals. At the end of the run Griffiths sat down and the conversation went:*
>
> *Griffiths: 'Did you hear many bullets pass you?'*
> *White (rather hot, tired and irritated): 'No, none.'*
> *Griffiths: 'Not many did you say?'*
> *White (fortissimo): 'No Griffiths, none!'*
> *Griffiths: 'Ah, not very many today.'*

The history of these mines is described in *Work of the RE in the European War 1914 - 1919. Military Mining.*

Two shafts, M1 and M2, were sunk close behind our front line trenches to a depth of about 12 feet [ie very shallow] and four feet six inches in square section. An old French shaft, M3, was also used. From these galleries, about 100 yards long, were driven forward and,

Entrance to a mining tunnel leading to the chamber under Hill 60, which were blown on April 17, 1915.

although the ground was good and hard, they were shored with frames and sheeting for protection against shake from shell fire. Ventilation was difficult and blacksmiths' bellows, fitted with rubber hosepipe, were used. Lighting was by candle. Spoil was removed on specially made silent trolleys running on wooden rails. The earth was filled into sandbags which were later built into the breastworks. Two chambers were excavated at the head of each gallery, in which the charges were placed. The charges in M1 and M2 were tamped with three ten feet thick sandbag walls with a ten feet air space between each. Both electrical and instantaneous fuze method of firing were duplicated. The enemy was heard working close to M3 on 2 April and it was feared that he might break into our gallery at any time. Work on the gallery was therefore suspended and a charge of 250 ponds (later increased to 500 pounds) of untamped gun cotton was laid as silently as possible.

When the mines were fired on 17 April debris flew 300 feet high and up to 300 yards away. It looked as if the inside of the hill was literally torn out. In view of later blows this view may appear exaggerated ; it accurately represents, however, the impression formed at the time. The chambers of M1 were about ninety feet apart, and

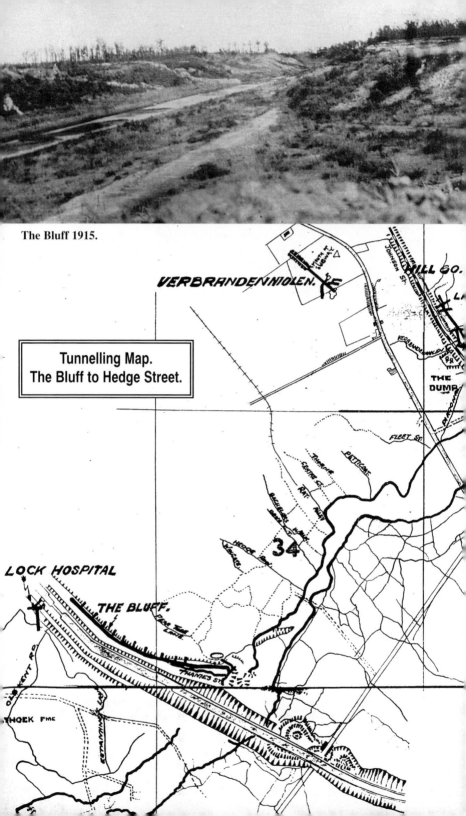

The Bluff 1915.

Tunnelling Map.
The Bluff to Hedge Street.

HILL 60 to the BLUFF

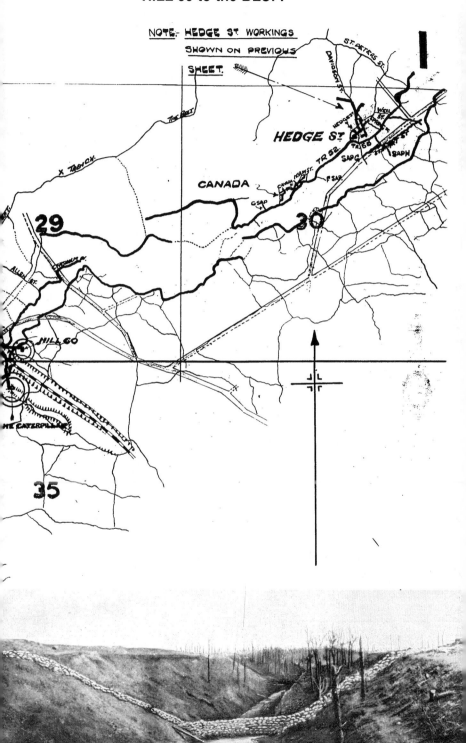

when fired they formed an enormous pit about ninety feet wide, 180 feet long and thirty feet deep. The craters formed in each of the two chambers of M2 and M3 were about thirty feet across. No one was allowed to enter the galleries after the blow until free of gas and the infantry were warned not to go down into the craters for at least half an hour after capture. Two sappers who entered M3 shaft without orders thirty six hours after the explosion were killed by gas due to the large amount of gun cotton used.

The day before the attack the Germans were again heard working very close to the junction of M3 and M3A, their intention being to blow up Trench 38; fortunately they were forestalled. One of the charges hung fire for two seconds; then some black substance appeared in the centre of the column of earth which was thrown up. This was possibly damp and unexploded powder. Our troops were warned to take cover from the debris; the curiosity of one man, who could not resist the very natural impulse to peer over the parapet to watch the effects of the mine exploding, cost him his life.

An examination of the captured enemy trenches disclosed a mine charged, tamped and complete with leads and an exploder, and one is left to speculate as to what the result would have been had the enemy got his blow in first.

The great mines on Hill 60 and the Caterpillar were commenced as far back as August 1915 - ie almost two years before they were actually See mining map on page 91-92 fired. Bulletin No 14 (1939) of the Tunnellers Old Comrades Association provides an account of the digging and setting of these mines and the conditions under which the Tunnelling Companies operated. The account that follows is taken from this journal, along with information from the Official History, Tunnellers, and Military Mining.

The effects of the strain of this class of work was always evident in the health of those involved, and it was found inadvisable to keep any one company in a particular position for more than about six months; accordingly in April 1916 the REs were relieved by a Canadian Tunnelling company. By this time it was evident that the war was not going to be won or lost in a matter of months, and the Canadians under Major North set out to put in two mines under two of the German strong points. In fact these were continuations of existing British workings, but after six months the Canadians had laid the two big mines under Hill 60 and the Caterpillar. The Gallery was driven forward 450 yards to two chambers, each about 90 feet below the ground surface. A charge of 45,700 pounds of ammonal plus 7,800

TABLE A

ORDER NORTH to SOUTH	NAME of MINE	% EFFICIENCY ENGLISH FORMULA	CHARGE LBS.	DEPTH in FEET	CIRCUITS and PRIMERS	METHOD of FIRING	DESIGN of CHAMBER	PACKING	TAMPING	DIAMETER AT GROUND LEVEL	WIDTH of RIM	DEPTH BELOW GROUND LEVEL	HEIGHT of RIM	DIAMETER OF COMPLETE OBLITERATION	AGE of CHARGE in MONTHS	REMARKS
2	Sᵗ ELOI	70	95,500 AMM 300 GLIC	125	THREE CIRCUITS - EACH 10 DETS EACH DET IN 13 3/8 STICK GELIC EACH PRIMER IN 50 LB AMM TIN	EXPLODER ON EACH CIRCUIT ALL FIRED TOGETHER	(diagram)	AMM TINS DETS BADLY ALTERNATELY	150 SOLID 10 Am·305 SOLID TOTAL 600 f³	176	77	17	8	330 NIL		THE DETONATORS WERE PLACED ALONG THE GALLERY AND WERE THUS NOT CENTRAL. THE MINE WAS 72½ DEEP IN "YPRESIAN" CLAY FOR WHICH THE SOIL FACTOR SHOULD HAVE BEEN 2 INSTEAD OF 1.7. THESE TWO POINTS DIRECTLY AFFECTED THE RESULT
3ᴮ	HOLLANDSCH ESCHUUR Nº2	76½	14,900 (12,500 Amm 2,400 BLAST)	58	TWO CIRCUITS - EACH 5 DETS ONE DET IN 50 LB DYN REST IN ONE ½ STICK DYN IN RUBBER BAG IN 50 AMM TIN	EXPLODER ON EACH CIRCUIT FIRED TOGETHER	(diagram)	AMM TINS DETS WELL SPACED	300 SOLID	105	55	14½	7	215	11	THIS CHARGE HAD PROBABLY DETERIORATED WHICH ACCOUNTS FOR ITS POOR RESULT
5	MAEDELSTEDE FM	80	94,000 (90,000 Amm 4,000 G.C.)	96	THREE CIRCUITS 12½% 12½% and 3ʳᵈ MAIN ½ TWO-EACH DET IN G.C. PRIMER IN 50 LB AMM TIN + THIRD-EACH DET IN 3" PIPE 15 LG - TWO WITH BLAST. ONE WITH GELIC	POWER ALL CIRCUITS	(diagram)	AMM TINS DETS WELL SPACED	350 SOLID 100 AIR TOTAL 570 f³	205	90	33	12	385 NIL	12	THE DETONATORS ON THE THREE CIRCUITS OF THIS CHARGE WERE NOT BALANCED, AND THIS PROBABLY ACCOUNTS FOR REDUCED RESULT
1ᴬ	HILL 60 A	91	53,500 (45,700 Amm 7,800 G.C.)	90	THREE CIRCUITS - EACH 5 DETS WITH EACH DET - 1 G.C. SLAB, 5 G.C. PRIMER IN 180 Am TIN AND 4 Nº8 DETS EACH PRIMER IN 180 Am T	POWER ALL CIRCUITS	(diagram)	4 GALLON PETROL TINS G.C. FILLING DETS BADLY-SPACED	90 SOLID 180 SOLID 200 AIR 605 Am TOTAL 630	191	47	33	11	285	10	THE DETONATORS OF THIS CHARGE WERE PLACED ALONG THE GALLERY. BETTER RESULTS WOULD HAVE BEEN OBTAINED IF THEY COULD HAVE BEEN PLACED CENTRALLY TO THE CHARGE
1ᴮ	HILL 60 B. CATERPILLAR	112	70,000 AMMONAL	85	THREE CIRCUITS - EACH 5 DETS EACH DET IN 1 G.C. SLAB 5 G.C. PRIMERS & 4 Nº8 DETS EACH PRIMER IN 180 A	POWER ALL CIRCUITS	(diagram)	4 GALLON PETROL TINS DETS WELL SPACED	100 AIR 180 SOLID TOTAL 6300 f³	260	60	51	17	360	10	DETONATORS PLACED ALONG CENTRAL PASSAGE OBTAINED GOOD RESULTS IN SPITE OF MANY SEPARATE CHAMBERS
1ᴮ	TRENCH 127 Nº6 Right	116½	40,000 AMMONAL	58	THREE CIRCUITS - EACH 6 DETS EACH DET IN 1 G.C. PRIMER WITH 10 Nº8 DETS IN 50 LB Amm TIN	EXPLODER ON ONE CIRCUIT ONLY	(diagram)	AMM TINS DETS WELL SPACED	420 SOLID	228	64	28	4	356	12	SEE REMARKS 10A
8ᴮ	KRUISSTRAAT Nº2	120½	30,000 AMMONAL	55	THREE CIRCUITS - EACH 6 DETS 9 IN 1 G.C. PRIMER WITH 10 Nº8 DETS 9 IN 1 STICKS G.C. DYN EACH PRIMER IN 50 LB	POWER ALL CIRCUITS	(diagram)	AMM TINS DETS WELL RIGHT ANGLE BEND	180 SOLID	217	75	40	10	367	11	GOOD ARRANGEMENTS SECURED GOOD RESULTS
4ᴬ	PETIT BOIS Nº2 Left	122	30,000 (21,000 Amm 9,000 BLAST)	50	TWO CIRCUITS - ONE LOST - EACH 6 DETS EACH DET IN 1 G.C. PRIMER WITH 8 Nº8 DETS	POWER REMAINING CIRCUITS ONLY	(diagram)	AMM TINS DETS SPACED	500 SOLID	217	100	46	4	417	10	Do / Do

DETAILS of CRATER in FEET — covers columns: DIAMETER AT GROUND LEVEL, WIDTH of RIM, DEPTH BELOW GROUND LEVEL, HEIGHT of RIM pounds of gun cotton was placed under Hill 60 (laid on 1 August 1916) whilst a charge of 70,000 pounds of ammonal was laid under the Caterpillar (completed 18 October 1916). At this point, almost at the close of 1916, the 1st Australian Tunnelling Company replaced the Canadians; their task was to protect these deep mines from German counter measures - mines which the Germans knew of, at least in general terms.

The two following stories of mining life on Hill 60 indicate something of its perilous nature. In 1997 I was able to spend some time in mining galleries which had not seen human activity in them for eighty years. They were comparatively clean, there was no danger from an enemy, but it was nevertheless a quite daunting experience and has given me renewed respect for the men who managed to endure the dangers of burrowing underground. They deserved their extra pay!

Major Ewan Tulloch was a member of both 171 and 175 Tunnelling Company. He describes an event that took place on Hill 60.

> *I decided the enemy was going to hole into one of our mine systems. I decided to build a barricade and wait until he had done so, with the intention of killing or capturing the miners and getting into their system. After about a week of listening to enemy mining at very close range, our officer always having to be on duty, complete with mobile charge, revolver and no lights. I decided to blow, and this was done. On making an examination afterwards we found there was a through draught of air from us*

Sappers and miners at work on a tunnel under Hill 60.

towards the enemy and no sign of the charge having broken through to the surface, so we naturally came to the conclusion that we were connected. Torches were used and a nasty-looking white box with German lettering on it was seen beyond some crushed casing. This could not be got out, so we decided to leave matters for a bit. Unfortunately, just as we were getting out of the mine an explosion occurred which killed a sapper on duty some distance from the box mentioned. The box, of course, had gone off, but did not do very much damage.

On 25 August 1915 an anonymous sapper officer serving with 46 (North Midland) Division had a very trying day. He was summoned in the very early hours of August 25 to come and deal with a problem at Hill 60; the Germans were heard under a new corner of Hill 60 and the local Brigadier, Kemp, wanted his advice. Instructions over the phone included the drilling of an 8 inch borehole down on top of the noises and awaiting arrival of the officer. He continues the story:

We made record time from Shrapnel Corner along the railway and up to 60. On arrival we found that they had only got down seven feet instead of the ten I wanted and that, alas, not over the loudest noise which was in a dugout about fifteen feet back from our front. I felt we had to get on, so we very soon had the roof off the dugout. It's funny how quickly men work when exposed from the knees upwards with Fritz about sixty yards away and dawn just breaking! Then we started the hole and were also stopped by a layer of flinty pebbles about seven feet down.

Luckily we found an iron bar and were able to punch the pebbles loose and collect them with the boring tool, making enough noise to be heard in Berlin, but it had to be done. When the hole was 12 feet down I left them to put 50 pounds of stuff in, tamp and fire, but to my horror nothing happened. It was a time fuze (which, by the way, I don't like). We pulled it out and found it had burnt to the end all right and the horrible idea forced itself on me that the Germans had found our charge and removed the stuff.

The only thing to be done was to remove the tamping and see, so the borer was set to work again and at last we saw the upper end of the zinc cylinder. Query: was there anything in it or not? Once more our iron bar came in handy and we drove its point through the zinc and it came up covered with Ammonal, to my relief. We then put three electric detonators in a five pound tin which we bedded down with about twenty pounds more and

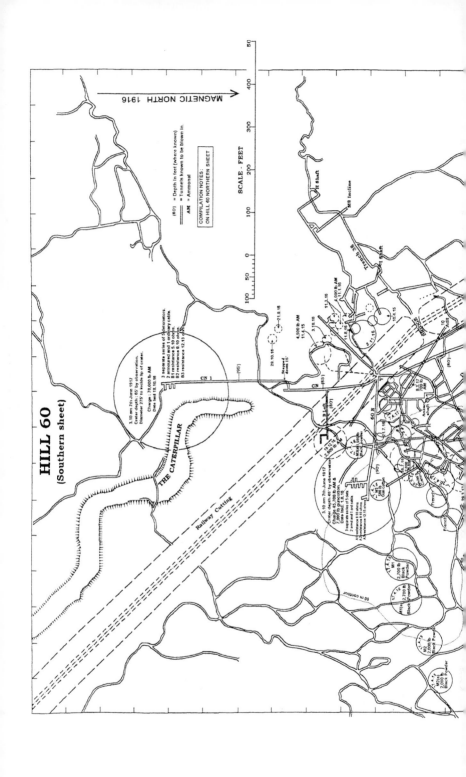

HILL 60
(Southern sheet)

MAGNETIC NORTH 1916

SCALE - FEET

(80') = Depth in feet (where known)
━━━ = Tunnels known to be blown in.
AM = Ammonal

COMPILATION NOTES:
ON HILL 60 NORTHERN SHEET

THE CATERPILLAR

3.10 am 7th June 1917
Crater depth: 65' by observation.
Diameter 275' to inside lip of crater.
Charge : 70,000 lb AM
Date laid 18.10.16

3 separate series of geophones.
B1 armoured and ordinary cable.
B1 resistance 5.10 ohms.
B2 resistance 9.10 ohms.
B3 resistance 12.13 ohms.

CN 1

(95')

CN (85')

Railway Cutting

3.10 am 7th June 1917
Crater depth: 45' by observation.
Charge 45,700 lb AM &
7,000 lb guncotton
Date laid 1.6.16

3 separate series of 5 sets.
2 armd and 1 ord cable.
A1 resistance ±10 ohms
A2 resistance ±10 ohms
A3 resistance 12.15 ohms

60 N

60 m contour

29.10.15

Stopped
down 15'

-21.9.15

4,500 lb AM
11.3.16

3.10.16

4,000 lb AM
11.1.16

11.3.16

11.8.16

10.4.15

5.7.15

Trench 38

H 6 Shaft

M/8 Incline

H Shaft

M1
2,700 lb Black Powder

M1(a)
2,700 lb Black Powder

M2
2,000 lb Black Powder

M2(a)
2,000 lb Black Powder

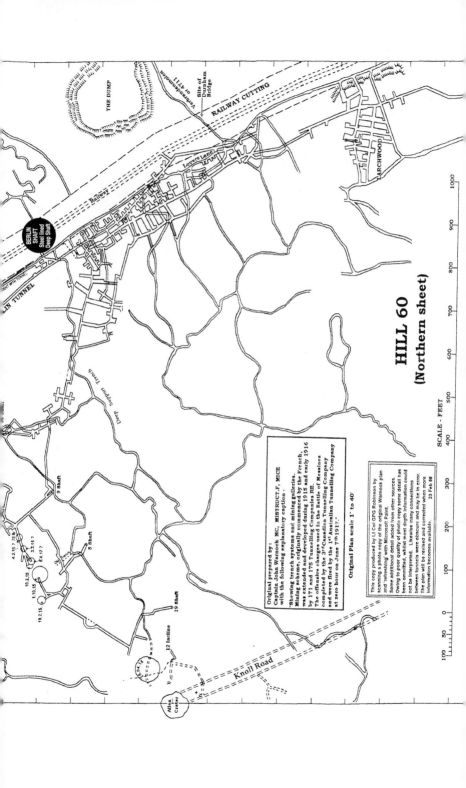

THE DUMP

Site of
Durham
Bridge

RAILWAY CUTTING

Verbrandenmolen

LARCHWOOD

Railway

Lover's Lane

BERLIN
SHAFT
Steel lined
Deep Shaft

IN TUNNEL

Deep Support Trench

9 Shaft

5 Shaft

4.2.15 7.70 5

3.2.15 7

10.2.15

8.4.17 7

1.10.15

19.2.15

19 Shaft

12 Incline

6.04.16

V=

W=

X=

Knoll Road

Alpha
Crater

HILL 60
(Northern sheet)

SCALE - FEET

100   50   0   100   200   300   400   500   600   700   800   900   1000

Original prepared by:
Captain John Warnock MC, MISTRUCT.F, MICE
with the following explanatory caption -

"Shewing trench systems and mining galleries.
Mining scheme, originally commenced by the French,
was extended and developed during 1915 and early 1916
by 171 and 175 Tunnelling Companies RE.
The offensive charges used in the Battle of Messines
completed by the 3rd Canadian Tunnelling Company
and were fired by the 1st Australian Tunnelling Company
at zero hour on June 7th 1917."

Original Plan scale 1' to 40'

This copy produced by Lt Col GPG Robinson by
scanning a photo copy of the original Warnock plan
and refreshing with Microsoft Paint.
Some additional detail added from other sources.
Owing to poor quality of photo copy some detail has
been ommitted, whilst most depth information could
not be interpreted. Likewise many connections
between tunnels were obscure and may be in error.
The plan will be revised and corrected when more
information becomes available.
                                        23 Feb 98

Tunnellers working in excellent conditions - almost certainly a posed photograph.

replaced the tamping and withdrew about thirty yards round the corner and let her go.

And he did go - we were busy dodging earth and sandbags for nearly a minute and then had to creep back to see the result which was a hole about thirty feet across and twelve deep. Now 75 pounds could never do that, so that the only conclusion was that our charge had succeeded in blowing up a much bigger German one under our feet - luckily for us at our time of choosing not at his.

175 Company took over from 171 in July 1915 and soon afterwards opened an adit (a horizontal opening into a mine) at rail level from the north side of the railway cutting about 220 yards behind the front line. Continuing on this level for some distance, the drive then descended on the incline, thereby greatly increasing the difficulty of penetrating the waterlogged sand. This and continuous fighting in the shallows, hindered progress, but after overcoming almost insuperable difficulties, the blue clay was at last reached, and the incline continued until it was ninety feet below the normal surface level. Known as the Berlin Tunnel, this mine became quite famous or infamous; it was specially detested by innumerable infantry working parties because of

the seemingly never ending amount of soil and water they had to remove from it.

Difficulties arose; in early 1916 a German miner, who had spent time at Hill 60, was captured on the Bluff; the Germans were planning to attack the right abutment of the railway bridge with a mine. The British reacted by digging a new gallery off to the right from the main drive, which in the meantime was halted, and fired a heavy camouflet, which removed the German threat, but also badly a few hundred feet of the Berlin Tunnel. On the other hand the British charge was fired just below a German deep shaft, and utterly wrecked their system.

Indeed, a German prisoner taken on the Somme some months later confirmed the effects of the blow. When the British charge was fired, no crater was formed; instead the explosion travelled along the German galleries and blew out a shaft in the shallow level. The ground was so bad that the Germans never succeeded in sinking a new shaft (this all on the Caterpillar side of the railway embankment). The ground of this side of the railway cutting was almost a bog, and in the attack of 7 June 1917 there were cases of men being actually engulfed in the morass, like a form of quicksand.

The 3rd Canadian Tunnelling Company relieved the 175th on this front and cleared up the damage; by far the majority of Berlin Tunnel (800 feet or so) was still intact. From here they broke off to the left to attack Hill 60 (60N) and another branch was started to the right to replace the one destroyed by the mine of 12 April 1916 (CN).

60 N proceeded without difficulty for some time until it ran into bad ground just before its objective; the problem was resolved by enlarging the proposed charge. However the ground was so bad that this chamber caved in, yellow clay appearing in the rush of water and slurry, indicating that this drive was almost out of the blue clay bed. The face was shored up and securely sealed against any further inrush, and a series of small chambers put in on each side of the drive; on completion of these 53,500 pounds of explosives were placed in position, detonators inserted and leads tested and registered. Owing to the scattered nature of the charge, extra precautions were taken to ensure speedy and complete detonation. The ammonal was placed in petrol tins and 7,800 pounds of gun cotton in slabs was packed into the spaces and then the whole was tamped - ninety feet solid, a hundred feet air, 180 feet solid, 200 feet air and sixty feet solid. This mine was known as Hill 60 A.

On the far side of the cutting the CN drive had run into bad ground and the face had collapsed. The galley was plugged and CN 1 was

Maintenance in the tunnels under Hill 60 was a never ending job. Note how the whole tunnel was supported by timber – an enormously expensive business.

started on the right, going down a further fifteen feet to get into firmer ground. Then it turned left and continued without interruption until it reached the German second line, well below the Caterpillar. By mid-August 1916 chambering commenced, swiftly followed by charging the mine with its explosives.

At this point disaster struck; the whole of the Berlin tunnel flooded, the charge was cut off by water and gas from a camouflet filled the mine. The cause of the flow of water was the construction of an intermediate gallery, D Break, driven to the left off the deep offensive incline. This gallery was fifty feet deep and intended to back up the shallow system. Bearing round to the right, it ran parallel to the main incline for some distance, then again curving under Trench 39 it

See map on page 95

became DR. Just behind Trench 39 a lateral was broken to the left, but had only advanced about ten feet when suddenly a rush of water burst in the face, flooding the workings, whilst the miners had a very narrow escape. It took several days of work on the pumps before an examination of the situation could be made.

The tunnellers had holed a damaged German gallery which had penetrated to a point some hundred feet behind the British line. The usual tools and sandbags and a portable electric lamp were found as well as an oxygen cylinder, presumably used to vent the system. By the end of August 230 feet of this German gallery had been recovered ad could then be used as a listening post, though a geophone could not be used because of the incessant dripping of water, which sounded through a geophone as if someone were working with a pick. Because of camouflets fired earlier, this part of their system was denied to the Germans. This extension of the British system became a key part of the underground battle; German countermining was observed from the heads of DLI and IDL, resulting in a British charge being fired at a time and place which would maximise the damage to the Germans and minimise it for the British workings. The psychology behind the British operations at this time was to keep the Germans concentrated on the shallows whilst great affairs went on in the bowels of the earth.

Meanwhile, the Caterpillar was fully loaded with the charge in water-tight tine. Special carrying parties were needed to handle so

Defensive Tunnelling under Hill 60.

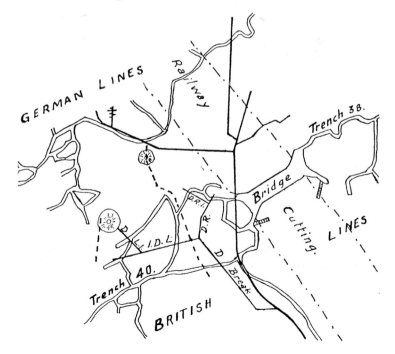

large a quantity of explosive. In order to ensure detonation three independent sets of leads were inserted in each charge, permitting nine circuits with no fewer than sixty detonators being distributed through the charges.

See Diagram on page 87

The mines had originally been intended (by General Allenby, when the project commenced commanding V Corps) to be fired at once, but now they were to await greater things.

Before the Canadians left Hill 60 they began work on a vertical, steel-lined shaft to replace the vulnerable long incline, which was called the Berlin Shaft. It was six feet in diameter and 94 feet deep. From the bottom a gallery was driven to the foot of the incline which drained the water back to a sump which was pumped up the shaft. This pumping not only made working conditions more acceptable, but had the added bonus of vastly improving the ventilation in the system. From the shaft also a new deep defensive system was dug, whilst an offensive gallery was started out towards the snout, a protuberance from the German line on the far side of Knoll Road.

See Map on page 91

German mining was not entirely harmless, and there were several scares. German camouflets, for example, on occasion trapped miners in the upper layers for several days. A new German shaft threatened the mine on Hill 60 itself, but the calculation was that the Germans would not get there before it was due to be fired - assuming that, for once, there was no postponement of the attack. The precise knowledge of the German rate of progress became known to the British in June 1915 when German galleries were broken into at Houplines; there it was noted that each shift recorded its progress on the timbers - which was a practice which the Germans carried out in all their galleries and right up to the end of the war.

Another problem was the periodic checks on the leads to the mines - galvanometer tests were taken regularly. To check these leads was a tremendous business, especially given the yards and yards of tamping that had been placed in the galleries leading to the chambers.

7 June 1917.

The Germans were well aware that something was up, and at Easter 1917 they made a large raid against the British trenches with the aim of destroying access to the underground workings. The details of the relatively minor effects of this may be seen in the accompanying reports. Further stretching of nerves was provided by the sound of a German shaft coming closer and closer to the A mine on Hill 60. It was trenches, etc, at HILL 60.

1. Front line and MARSHALL WALK knocked out - a few
   points in deep support trench being held also shell
   holes.
2. Mine system not entered.
3. SWIFT STREET to Deep Infantry dug-outs crumped in and
   being repaired also some dug-outs crumped in.
4. Nearly all stairways crumped also some of the dug-outs
5. Enemy reported to have got into deep dug-outs and to
   have entered old Tunnelling Officers' dug-outs and
   wireless room but not to have got into BERLIN TUNNEL
6. 2 Australian Sergts. and 5 (?) O.R. missing.
7. Enemy bombed deep dug-outs from MARSHALL WALK.
8. LARCH WOOD TUNNEL - some caps broken.
9. LARCH WOOD dug-outs alright.
10. Enemy left yellow flags at entrance to Infantry
    dug-outs in MARSHALL WALK and reached a point about
    250 yards from bridge along cutting.
11. Enemy had been bombarding all day from 8 a.m.
12. The enemy was in our trenches an hour.

a.g.ste (signature)

Lieut. Colonel. R.E.
Controller of Mines.
Second Army.

10/4/1917.

a blast from this that damaged the leads to the mine, which required
immediate repair. A member of the company continues the saga:

*By this time we felt that we were at breaking point and it is
doubtful how much longer we could have held out had not the
order come to prepare to blow. Although no date was fixed we
knew it was to be soon, and all preparations were made.*

To Controller of Mines.

From O.C. 1st Australian Tunnelling Company.

Early on the morning of the 9th inst. the enemy opened with heavy bombardment of minerwerfers and continued throughout the day increasing in intensity about 6-30 ; guns of all calibre being used. This was followed by an enemy raiding party. Although the bombardment was severe comparatively little damage was done to the underground workings.

The INFANTRY TUNNEL near the connection of "A" dug-out was crumped for a distance of about 100' cutting off communication between the Infantry tunnel dug-outs and Company Headquarters and Swift Street This also stopped communication with the shallow underground workings.

The SWIFT STREET exit was blown by minerwerfer and the fumes filled the Gallery. This caused a panic amongst the Infantry, who despite the Proto Men's orders to get out of the Gallery resulted in about 30 being gassed all of which with the exception of five or six died.

The enemy entered the dug-outs near the old spiral stairs and made what appears to have been a thorough search of the old tunnellers headquarters. The enemy entered and bombed the wireless dug-out ; the operator however succeeded in destroying his instrument. Enemy also bombed the old petrol engine without doing any material damage. Most the exits were partially or wholly destroyed. The corner of the Subway near the "G" Exit was also crumped. Larchwood Subway was crumped in three places and communication interrupted for a little time.

The enemy bombed our store without doing material damage also bombed cookhouse and Sergeant's Dug-out which open on to Marshall Walk doing slight damage. Both entrances to Infantry dug-outs from Marshall Walk were destroyed by enemy's mobile charges. Larchwood Subway repaired and Communication re-established. Exits from Infantry Tunnel are also repaired. Repairs to subway between "A" Dug-out to Swift Street have abandoned and new gallery being driven. This gallery will run into a large crater which will have to be crossed and sandbagged overhead. T dead end from "B" dug-out Infantry Tunnel will be continued some little distance, and will then turn off and connect up between the new proto house and Company Headquarters as per slip tracing. Dug-outs will be off this later.

The front line from the bridge to Allen Street has practical all been destroyed, Swift Street, Metropolitan and Bensham Road being a like condition. Number 10 Adit has not yet been located.

ANZAC Shaft has been inspected and is in good condition.

No.13 Shaft has not yet been located. No.9 shaft is in good order. None of the Shallow Workings have been inspected yet but an attempt will be made by Proto men tonight.

"H" & "I"s. These shafts have been crumped in and it is as yet impossible to locate them owing to the front line being blotted out Trench 35 is in the same plight.

(Sgd) J.Douglas Henry. Major. A.E.

Exploders were connected to the three electric leads and a master switch was installed to connect alternatively all the three leads to an engine used for lighting.

The day approached and Major Henry (the OC) was called to

GHQ (of the Army) where he was issued with a specially synchronised watch. We knew then our vigil was nearly over. Three switches and the master switch were in place; the three exploders were connected and the engine running well. If the engine failed then any one of the three exploders could have done the job. All preparations complete, Major Henry and the three officers retired to the dugout where the exploders were connected in readiness.

It is difficult to describe that last half hour. A beautiful, clear starlit night - as calm a night from a bombardment point of view as ever had existed on that much contested front. An occasional Very light fell like a bright meteorite and a lone occasional crack of a rifle.

Ten minutes to go. How are you feeling? Fine, thank you, Sir, This is our great occasion! Yes, Sir. Eight minutes, still clear outside - one gun fires, then silence.

When do you get leave? Next week with luck. Five minutes now. All quiet. Wonder what Fritz is doing? Will he beat us to it? Has he heard about it and withdrawn?
Get ready boys. One minute only.

Someone asks: 'Can I have this switch Major when it's over for a souvenir?' 40 seconds. Yes, you can, and you other two can have the others. 3 seconds to go. What about the watch, major? 20 seconds to go. That is mine. Get ready. 10 seconds, 9, 8, 7, 6,

Crater of mine exploded at Hill 60 on 7 June 1917. Zillebeke Lake can be seen in the distance.

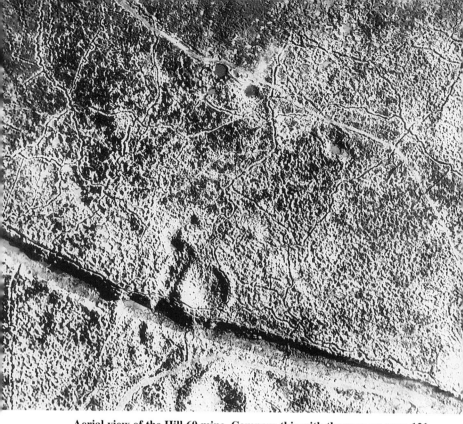

Aerial view of the Hill 60 mine. Compare this with the map on page 121.

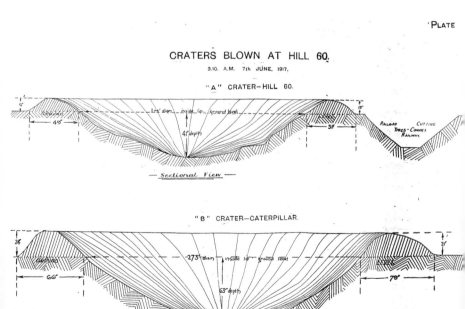

'PLATE

CRATERS BLOWN AT HILL 60.

3.10. A.M. 7th JUNE, 1917,

"A" CRATER—HILL 60.

— Sectional View —

"B" CRATER—CATERPILLAR.

— Sectional View —

5, 4, 3, 2, 1, FIRE.

Simultaneously with the pressing of the master switch by Captain Woodward, other switches were thrown on other parts of the front, and while the material from the explosion was still high in the air, every gun on the British front opened fire.

Pandemonium - hell on earth let loose.

Hanging on the wall in the Imperial Service Club in Sydney can be seen a small electric switch, neatly mounted on a piece of cedar, which is a vivid reminder of that great day in the history of the 1st Australian Tunnelling Company.

The Master of Belhaven was with his guns at Zillebeke.

At exactly 3.10 am Armageddon began. The timing of all batteries in the area was wonderful, and to a second every gun roared in one awful salvo. At the same moment the two greatest mines in history [actually they weren't, but he can be forgiven the hyperbole] *were blown up - Hill 60 and one immediately to the south of it* [ie the Caterpillar] *I cleared everyone out of the dugouts and was watching for it. Never could I have imagined such a sight. First, there was a double shock that shook the earth here 5,000 yards away like a gigantic earthquake. I was nearly flung off my feet. Then an immense wall of fire that seemed to go half way up to heaven. The whole country was lit with a red light like in a photographic dark-room. At the same moment all the guns spoke and the battle began on this part of the line. The noise surpasses even the Somme; it is terrific, magnificent, overwhelming. It makes one almost drunk with exhilaration, and one does not care about the fact that we are under the concentrated fire of all the Hun batteries. Their shells are bursting round now as I write, at 3.40 am, but it makes one laugh to think of their feeble little efforts compared to 'ausgezeichnete Ausstellung' that we are providing. We are getting our revenge for 1914 with a vengeance. It is now beginning to get light, but the whole world is wrapped in a grey haze of acrid fumes and dust.*

The attack by the infantry here went through with little loss; indeed the attack could have been pressed on to far greater depths, so great was the disorganisation of the Germans. However, the plan did not allow for this; by 14 June all objectives had been taken. The line in this sector had been advanced about 1500 yards, including the whole of Battle Wood.

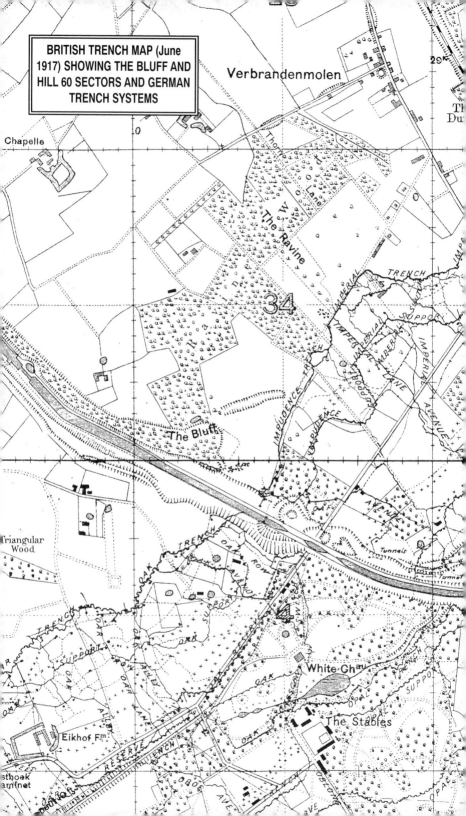

BRITISH TRENCH MAP (June 1917) SHOWING THE BLUFF AND HILL 60 SECTORS AND GERMAN TRENCH SYSTEMS

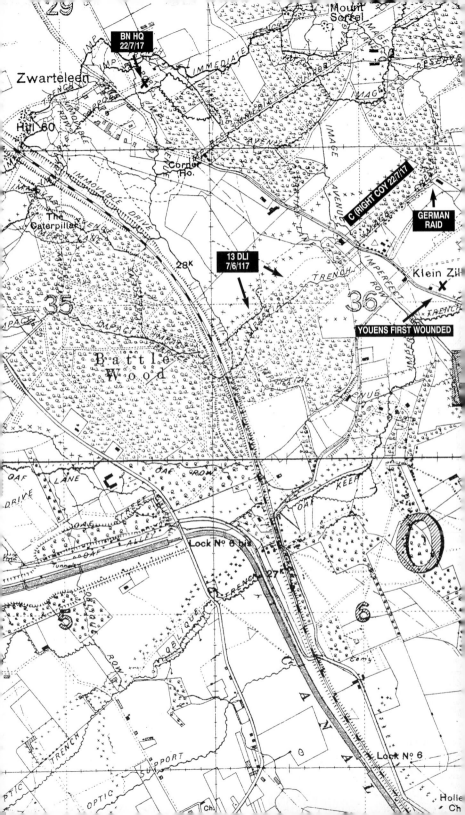

29

Mount Sorrel

BN HQ
22/7/17

Zwarteleen

Hill 60

Corner
Ho.

The
Caterpillar

28ᴷ

13 DLI
7/6/117

C (RIGHT COY 22/7/17

GERMAN
RAID

Klein Zil

36

YOUENS FIRST WOUNDED

35

Battle
Wood

OAF LANE

OAF ROW

OAF
DRIVE

OAF KEEP

Lock Nº 8 bis

27ᴷ

5

6

Lock Nº 6

Holle
Ch

The last of the Hill 60 VCs: Second Lieutenant F Youens

13/DLI were part of the 23rd Division, which was the division that captured the Hill 60 sector in the Messines attack. 13/DLI were in reserve for this attack, south of Zillebeke Lake, but that night moved up to Impartial Trench, having covered the ground en route that had cost both sides so much blood and effort over the preceding three years or so.

They remained in the area for some time, and it was during the enhanced period of tension that followed Messines, but before the main offensive proper began, that Second Lieutenant Youens won his VC.

At 12.15 am on 7 July, Second Lieutenant Frederick Youens and three men left the right of the battalion front to get into touch with the troops on that flank. A strong party of Germans endeavoured to surround and capture this small patrol, but after a fight, in which Youens and one man were wounded, the Durhams regained their own lines. Soon a fierce bombardment fell upon the trenches of the 13th and about 2.30 am some 50 Germans attempted to raid the right company. A shell burst scattered one Lewis gun team, but Second Lieutenant Youens, who was receiving medical aid in a dugout, rushed forth without shirt or jacket and rallied the men. A bomb was thrown amongst them, but he hurled it out of the trench. Another came and this also he seized; but it exploded in his hands, wounding him so seriously that he died. The German raid failed, and this gallant young officer was awarded the Victoria Cross.

Second-Lieutenant F Youens, V.C.

Youens was born in 1893 in High Wycombe and gained a scholarship to Grammar school. The school magazine, in its obituary, said of him:

He died as he had lived, a man of the highest ideals, of indomitable courage, and with a total disregard of self.

In 1914, while teaching at Rochester (at St Peter's School), he gained a scholarship tenable at Oxford University.

He came from a not particularly well-off background, as is illustrated by his scholarship career, and the need for him to

See Ma
pag
103

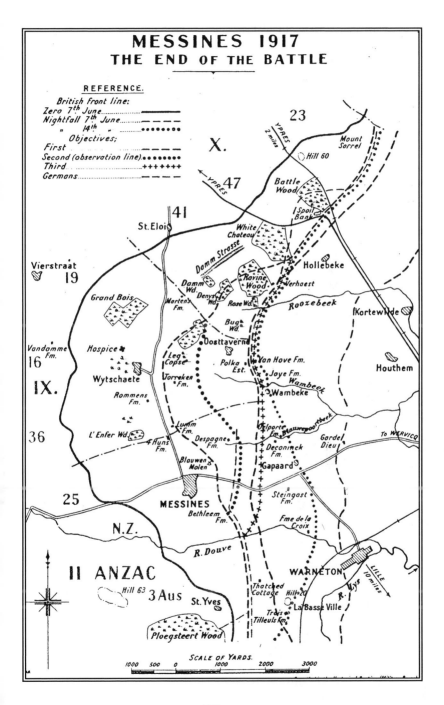

MESSINES 1917
THE END OF THE BATTLE

REFERENCE.

British front line:
Zero 7th June...............
Nightfall 7th June.......
    "   14th   "   ....
Objectives;
First.............................
Second (observation line)........
Third.............................++++++++
Germans..........................

X.

23

2 miles YPRES

Hill 60

Mount Sorrel

47

YPRES 2 miles

Battle Wood

41

St. Eloi

White Chateau

Spoil Bank

Damm Strasse

Ravine Wood

Hollebeke

Damm Wd.

Denys Wd.

Verhaest

Vierstraat

19

Grand Bois

Martens Fm.

Rose Wd.

Roozebeek

Kortewilde

Vandamme Fm.

16

Hospice

Bug Wd.

Oosttaverne

Leg Copse

Van Hove Fm.

Houthem

IX.

Wytschaete

Torreken Fm.

Polka Est.

Joye Fm.

Wambeek

36

Rommens Fm.

Wambeke

L'Enfer Wd.

Lumm Fm.

Elporte Fm. Blauwepoortbeek

Gardel Dieu

To WERVICQ

4 Huns Fm.

Despagne Fm.

Deconinck Fm.

25

Blauwen Molen

Gapaard

Steingast Fm.

MESSINES

Bethleem Fm.

Fme de la Croix

N.Z.

R. Douve

WARNETON

LILLE 10 miles

II ANZAC

Hill 63

3 Aus

St. Yves

Thatched Cottage

Hill 20

La Basse Ville

R. Lys

Trois Tilleuls Fm.

Ploegsteert Wood

SCALE OF YARDS.

1000 500 0 1000 2000 3000

work before he could gain entrance at Oxford. When the war began he joined the RAMC as a Private, from which he transferred to 7/East Surrey in 1915. He was severely wounded whilst serving with them; he did not fully recover until late in 1916. He was gazetted to B/DLI in February 1917, having avoided the temptation to take a home posting, and went to France in that month.

He is buried in Railway Dugouts (Transport Farm) Cemetery in I.O.3

1. 'There were still two mines of 30,000 pounds each unexploded. These lay to the south, and had been reserved for firing on the second day of the battle, to extend our right flank. But the precipitate retreat of the enemy, exceeding the wildest hopes of our staff, rendered them unnecessary.

For the rest of that year, and well on into 1918, we were in correspondence with the Belgian Government, through the Belgian Mission and the General Staff, over the question of the removal of these mines. Now it is one thing to put a mine down into blue clay, but it is even more difficult to recover the gallery and charges months afterwards, when the heavy pressure experienced in such ground would have broken up all timbering. It was therefore agreed that a careful survey should be made of the position of the shafts and that the charges would be removed later on, when the pressure of work on the Tunnelling Companies should be less heavy. Neat concrete bench marks were erected, and everyone was happy. But when the Germans made their great drive on Hazebrouk in 1918, we naturally took the opportunity of declining any further responsibility for the twins, as we called them, and as far as I know these babies are still beneath the sod, and may they ever remain there.' (Unfortunately one has since exploded, in July 1955, but no one was hurt.)

Further information comes from *Tunnellers*, Captain W Grant Grieve and Bernard Newman. reprinted by Naval and Military Press. nd

The Durham Forces in the Field 1914 - 1918, Vol II, Captain Wilfred Miles. Cassell 1920. The DLI Museum is publishing this year (1998) a brief history of all its VC winners, *Beyond all Praise*. I am also grateful to that museum, and the curator, Mr Steve Shannon, for permission to use copies of the pocket book version of the Battalion War Diary.

The war diary notebook of 13/DLI, recording Youens' action,

x Dispositions Map #144 60.
HQrs. I.29.d.6.4.
C Coy. I.36. b.2.0 to
I.36. b. 5.8
B I.36. b 5.8 to I 30.d. 15.60.
D I.30. c.75.65.
A I.29. d. 4.4.
Casualties. 1.OR. wounded

7.8.17. 12.15 AM. A patrol consisting of 2/Lt Youens and 3 OR left the right of Battn front to get into touch with the 17th LONDON REGT. They then proceeded to about I.36. b.5.1. were a party of 40 of the enemy were observed carrying material into the strong point. The enemy covering party tried to surround the patrol after a bombing fight our patrol was forced to retire. 2/Lt

YOUENS. & NCO being wounded. 145 AM to 3 AM. Enemy shelled front and support lines very heavily. 2.30 AM. a party of about 60 Germans attempted to raid the right coy at I.36. b.5.8. They were repulsed with rifle and Lewis gun fire. 2/Lt Youens altho wounded came out of the dugout without turning or shirt and rallied a L.G. team which had been disorganised by a shell. The enemy threw a bomb into the centre of this L.G. team and 2/Lt YOUENS caught hold of it and threw it away. The enemy did this a second time and as 2/Lt YOUENS was throwing the second bomb away it burst badly wounding him. Enemy artillery normal.

Chapter Four

THE GERMANS AT HILL 60: THE EXPERIENCE OF 105th RESERVE INFANTRY REGIMENT

For this part of the book I am, once more, indebted to the hard labour of Ralph Whitehead in the USA. He has also taken the trouble to provide much of the accompanying photography. Seeing something from the other side of the trench is always an important balance, and certainly the descriptive writing of von der Gabelentz is extremely powerful. Although I have placed most of the text to indicate that it is a quote, I have been quite free with the adaptation of the translation and have edited out parts as necessary, most particularly that relating to individuals.

From the middle of December 1914 until June 1915 the sector from the Caterpillar (known to the Germans as Hill 59) through to Zandvoorde was held by the 105th RIR (Reserve Infantry Regiment), a formation roughly equal to a three battalion brigade in the British army. It was also known as 6th Royal Saxon Infantry Regiment, King

Germans in a rear trench in the Hill 60 area.

William II of Württemburg. It had had a very hard time in the fighting, being reduced to twenty officers and about nine hundred other ranks, ie about a quarter of its proper size, by mid November. In the fighting at First Ypres it took part in battles with the French, for the most part, losing heavily at Hollebeke Chateau, Verbrandenmolen and the Bluff. Whilst there is not time for it here, it is interesting to note in the history the records of hiring and firing amongst divisional commanders, the disputes between Army Groups (Linsingen and Fabeck) and between smaller formations - for example the failure of the 2nd Cavalry Division to provide manpower to help with the occupation of a vital part of the canal, which was to become known to history as the Bluff.

On 16 December the Regiment took over the Hill 60 sector; the rear billets were at Tenbrielen and the battle headquarters were in a farmstead west of Hollebeke Chateau. The Regiment came under the command of the 30th Division.

> *The position was poorly developed and severely shot up. In the consistently flat countryside, Hill 60 offered an excellent observation position up to Ypres and upon the overall enemy positions; however, as a result of this it drew all the more concentrated enemy fire upon itself. So, in the truest sense of the word, the possession of this 'outstanding' observation position in the flat countryside was of the most supreme importance for both sides. If the German artillery was to benefit from it, it was dependent on the bravery of the battle-proven 105th Regiment.*

> *Hill 60 became indelibly connected with the history of the Regiment while it fought in Flanders as a consequence of bitter fighting, the highest bravery and glory and the very heavy losses. It ranks along with the achievements at Gheluvelt, Hooge, Douamont, Verdun, Sailly Saillisel and the tank battle at Cambrai, but it was here that the losses were heaviest. It was capable of standing firm with a stubborn resistance to the wearing out effect resulting from the serious enemy fire and the inevitable daily heavy losses.*

On 20 December the line of the Regiment was extended to the Caterpillar and on the 21st to the woods just east of Zwarteleen. The first days in the line were hectic - after the first two days the troops in the forward line had to be relieved.

> *There they lay under heavy enemy fire which caused serious losses to the troops who were hard at work at night constructing positions, mainly breastworks* [ie, the equivalent of trenches above ground created by using sandbags] *which were continually*

Skizze 2.

Höhe 59 u. 60.

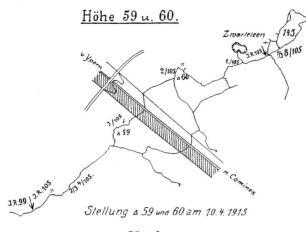

Stellung △ 59 und 60 am 10. 4. 1915.

Skizze 3.

Höhe 60.

———— Gehaltene Stellung.
··········· Verlorene Stellung.
·—·—·— Neue Sturmausgangsstellung

Nach der Sprengung: Stellung am 17. 4. 1915.

Skizze 4.

Höhe 60.

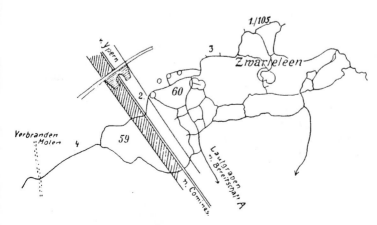

Stellung am 15. 5. 1915.
○ ○ ○ 3 alte Sprengtrichter.

German map showing the various stages of the fighting at Hill 60. April-May 1915.

being destroyed by the enemy's artillery. The relief of front, support and reserve troops continued on a two day basis until the end of December; the routine consisted of daily enemy wearing out fire, retaliation fire because of small raids on our side, small mine explosions from both sides, drum fire on 27 December for the preparation of two enemy attacks which were stifled in the bud by our fire and on 29 December there was an explosion at a forward driven sap, that cost III/105 [ie the third battalion of the Regiment] 3 dead and 12 wounded. We had our first Christmas in the field and did not disturb the enemy.

In early January the Regiment moved to Menin as Army Reserve, and there received a massive draft of almost sixteen hundred men and officers. Now reinforced, the Regiment took over more trenches to the right. They returned to this sector on 12 January.

The positions on the heights of the Caterpillar and Hill 60 were now well developed, the enemy fire had become quieter, on the other hand the positions in Zwarteleen and more and more to its right, [called by the Germans] Saubacht, were seriously crumbling, and only with a considerable effort were they maintained in a defensible condition, not least because of the high ground water level. A covered approach to Hill 60 was

German soldier relaxing by a shelter. Note the barbed wire and supports on top of the trench wall.

constructed by the pioneers during the rest period of the Regiment, so that now the reliefs were protected by it, and it no longer had to take place over the open embankment.

The Germans also used mine warfare defensively. A group of houses in front of the Zwarteleen sector were targeted because it was feared that the British (who had now arrived on Hill 60) would do so if the Germans did not. The mine was fired at 6.15 am on a dank February morning. The German troops

occupied the mine crater, in which some Englishmen from the East Yorkshire Regiment were buried, and they developed it. The enemy was apparently entirely surprised and first began fighting against the German position after 7 am with machine gun fire, and soon also with artillery fire. At 8 am a strong enemy hand grenade attack took place against the new crater position which collapsed under defensive fire, but there were heavy casualties. The forward line was reinforced, but the new crater line was evacuated because it was not intended to occupy it permanently.

March proved to be an interesting time.

Meanwhile pioneer officers at our positions on the Caterpillar and Hill 60 made extensive investigations for sites for gas cylinders for a gas attack; they were installed by 12

March. The troops in the front line received anti-gas respirators and instructions on how to act in the case of the gas being released because of damage to the cylinders by shell fire.

On 12 March a mine was blown under the last remnants of the group of houses which were so heavily fought over; and finally to end enemy mining activity in the Zwarteleen sector. At 5.30 am a mine of 2700 pounds was fired which blew away the remnants of the houses and trenches to a width of a hundred metres and a gigantic mine crater, as deep as a house, emerged at the

A posed photograph of German soldiers. Note the stick grenades on the soldier on the right.

position. It was not intended that the position should be occupied by our force, but it was also to be denied to the enemy, so they placed a heavy artillery bombardment in and around the new crater and troops dug a sap up to the edge of the mine crater in their front in order to be able to overlook it and dominate it.

Preparations for the gas attack continued, the opening of the offensive being scheduled for 23 March; this was postponed, because of unfavourable wind which sprang up during the night, leaving hundreds of troops packed into the forward area. The next attack date, 29 March, also passed without action; again because of the wind. It was postponed to the 30th and then to the 31st, but in the end was cancelled at midday on that date. It is nice to know that the Germans had their problems with the weather! A neighbouring Corps was to try gas on 15 April, but the wind was unfavourable again. In the midst of all this tension and preparation for an offensive came the British attack on 17 April.

See Chapter 1 page 20 onward. *Then, on the evening of 17 April, shortly after 8 pm* [British 7 pm], *the companies in Kortewilde felt a violent earth tremor, a deafening blast was heard coming to the rear from the forward line, everyone rushed out into the open and strained to listen, but they only saw a huge, monstrous, yellowish-black, thick smoke mushroom cloud that covered the entire position of the Regiment on Hill 60. No one knew what had happened, however, until the violent and audible noise of battle reached there from the front line. Everyone now knew what had happened, exactly what the troops stationed there had always feared and of whose reports about enemy mine-working no one ever took seriously, whether at higher formation level or even the pioneers, whose job it was to conduct counter-mine work.*

The blast had almost completely obliterated the position of 2/105 on Hill 60 by three mine explosions [actually five] *that had*

been set with great accuracy under the trenches of the front line. This was now followed by an impenetrable curtain of heavy fire; iron and smoke covered the earth on the entire position of the Regiment and its lines connecting it to the rear, especially that on the whole of Hill 60. The English infantry advanced as almost the entire garrison of the front line was blasted into the air, so that after the battle the top of the hill was transformed and occupied by a huge mine crater, and about a hundred metres beyond it into the communication trench.

The Germans made heroic attempts to stem the attack. Attempts by neighbouring men to restore the situation were doomed to failure, because the heart had been blown out of the position and all cohesion was lost, with no-one knowing what the situation was on Hill 60. All that could be done was to ensure that the British did not break out any further from the Hill 60 sector.

Then a greater problem emerged - that of the gas canisters. Nearly all the officers were casualties, and when the most senior, Leutnant der Reserve Steinmann, was wounded and evacuated to the rear,

a panic arose in the exhausted men of 2/105, already shattered by the explosion and their heavy casualties in the defensive battle, because a rumour spread among them that the gas cylinders that were among them had been destroyed in the explosions, and that gas was moving forward into the German positions. Large numbers of men ran away to the rear positions, terrified at the prospect of being gassed, and to the supports at the railway embankment.

The situation was restored by Oberstleutnant [Lieutenant-Colonel] Furstenau. He was a most formidable man, who had lost his arm in an early stage of the war, but had persuaded the authorities to allow him back to his beloved Regiment. His headquarters had received no information about leaking gas and ordered the men to be gathered and returned to the front line. Meanwhile nothing more could be done other than to block the enemy with the support company.

The 30th Division gave orders that the height position was irreplaceable as an artillery observation post and must be taken back at any cost. He was given reinforcements of another brigade equivalent of men, with the main thrust of the attack to be launched from Zwarteleen.

At 12.10 am [British time] attacks were launched from the Caterpillar, from the new front on Hill 60 and from Zwarteleen. The frontal attack did not succeed *it made only a little headway, for when the attackers left their protection they were smashed by the enemy's fire, as they had already succeeded in installing numerous machine guns* [in actual fact four, and not on this side; here there were one, plus the QVR gun from the other side of the bridge which might have had an impact] *into the side of the crater just before the attack. Their cone of bullets mowed down the attackers when they left their trenches and forced them into the rear into their heavily damaged trenches.*

The fighting degenerated into a bombing match.

This hindered the massing of more forces as the hand grenades were useful but at that time the infantry had had insufficient training in their use and the use of pioneers as throwers was necessary.

From Zwarteleen the attack had limited success. Those who had crept forward to the craters had been forced back and were obliged to put a block into their trench. Another attempt was made when the reinforcements came up,

they made it to the edge of the hill position, only a few metres from the crater's edge, where any British soldier unlucky enough to be close to this point could scarcely have avoided any quick shot of ours. However all efforts here were ruined with the brilliantly aimed artillery barrage of the British, which cut off their weak point and caused numerous casualties to these men.

Attempts to continue this attack failed - indeed all the company officers were now casualties, and the men no longer had the heart for the attack, although they did hold and strengthen their position.

At the end of the day the situation had been stabilised, but it was not comfortable, and the 30th Division still wanted the British removed.

At 4.15 am [British time] *a new attack was launched with 'all the forces available',*

This assault also brought no real progress in spite of an energetic advance as the captured ground could not be held because of the heavy losses...The first attacks carried forward from Zwarteleen also broke entirely in the enemy's machine gun fire, assisted by an English Very light that set fire to the ruins of a house in Zwarteleen so that the bright flames illuminated the advancing troops from the rear.

Losses were well over 300 for 105 Regiment alone.

The Germans set about recovering and regrouping; new mine galleries were pushed forward from the Caterpillar as listening points (no less than fourteen of them) and camouflet charges were prepared on the right of the position. Meanwhile more and more British artillery was being removed northwards, to deal with the German offensive that had been launched there; in anyy case, some of the urgency of the situation had been taken out of Hill 60 as it was evident that the British had not discovered any canisters of gas.

An attack against Hill 60 and so called double Hill 60 was ordered on 1 May. Double Hill 60 was the British Hill 62 and a prominence to its south, just below Observatory Ridge. Gas cylinders were opened on 1 May, and patrol activity became very heavy; the orders for the attack were to take and hold these high positions.

At 8.45 the order is given to open the cylinders at 9 [both British time]. *At 9.05 60 small and five large cylinders in 105's sector* [ie opposite Hill 60 and on the Caterpillar] *are opened. During the release of the gas the wind changed there and the gas cloud, that was about ninety metres wide, encountered only a small part of the foremost British positions; the enemy could easily avoid the cloud by moving sideways.*

It also floated, as a consequence of the unfavourable wind, over the German positions and caused casualties by gas poisoning, especially in the support company. About forty of them became casualties. The attackers reached the double mine crater on Hill 60,

however they were forced to go to fall back to the south edge of the mine crater because of the enemy's machine gun fire from the flanks, the heavy artillery fire that fell just forward of the crater and the violent hand grenade attack in the front line area from a superior enemy force. The attack had only casualties, as no gain had been made; still a lesson was learned from the failure, that a gas attack must be made on a wider front so as to be able to avoid a flanking attack by the enemy. Also the storm troopers must be placed in position further to the rear and that the respirators were inadequate.

The story of the attack on Hill 60 itself on 5 May is given in a graphic account by Georg von der Gabelentz, who is most extraordinarily anti-English. He starts by tracing the events prior to the great attack.

This time the Englishmen, coloured and white, had dug themselves in opposite them and a battle was fought between two foes that was ferocious and full of hatred because they knew that the souls of the tradesmen over there were to thank for this

*war of death and horror and unending agony. The expression,
'Gott Strafe England', had entered into the hearts of everyone.
They could never know at home of the ghastly carnage and the
warm blood of your neighbour that sprays in the face of
comrades and friends causing such hatred! In the evening of one
April day the Englishmen blew up part of our fire trench on Hill
60 into the air. Many a good man was blown apart and buried.
There was furious fighting and it was fought with rugged bravery
on both sides. There is no quarter given - Gott Strafe England!
The battle wavered back and forth for days. A small mistake
would allow victory to be gained by either side.*

The day came for the attack, 5 May.

*A spring day came over Flanders. The larks sang as they
never have before, the sun tempted the first spring flowers from*

**A German trench to the rear of Hill 60 - this one is in unnaturally
immaculate condition!**

a soil fertilised with blood. First of all the companies that were specified for the attack were moved slightly back so that the artillery could work against the English trenches unobstructed, as the trench lay only a stone's throw from ours. The synchronised clocks in the German dugouts indicated it was the fourth hour since the artillery had opened fire on the English trenches. The larks suddenly grew quiet. The black projectiles of our mortars roared down upon the bare ground that covered the English trenches, like hammers hitting in a steel factory. Soon the land was shrouded in a cloud of dust and suffocating vapours.

See Chapter 2 page 55 onwards

The telephone in the command dugout rings. A message comes from an artillery observation post in front which says that the effect of the mortars is favourable. Favourable? To the devil! Even the most stubborn Englishman can no longer be alive in such an iron hail. The enemy artillery is not quiet, their artillery shells patter and crash on the German lines and between here and over there the iron messengers howl and frightened little birds flutter, suddenly interrupted in their love song. They whizz here and there, finding neither rest nor protection and finally fall to the ground from fatigue or torn to pieces by the iron vultures.

Wires are cut and repaired; the attacking troops hug the trench walls so that they are moderately protected. The waiting is interminable. The commander fortifies those around him with red wine and cigars.

Twilight covered the land, and finally the time for the assault comes. The German artillery, punctual to the minute, places their fire to the rear of the British forward positions, barrage fire to spoil the advance of the English reserves, and then our men break forth with a cheer. In an instant they whisk into the English trench, where there follows a terrible turmoil. Hand grenades crash, a great chaos reigns, man hurls himself against man, rifle butts and spades swing through the air, blades flash up and plunge into men's bodies, murderous eyes glisten with the lust of victory, feet pound, gasps, yells, groans. The fallen lie on the ground and use their teeth or try to strangle each other. Very lights flare up and tremble with their ghostly lustre about the wild turmoil. The hours go by, already it is midnight. Their loved one's might sleep peacefully in their homes whilst the wildest fighting still rages here, and only the quiet lie down, those that will never again open their eyes in the morning.

Never ending message upon message flies toward the support positions. 'Send hand grenades forward immediately.' Then an emotional voice, 'Rifle ammunition is running out! Quickly, send ammunition forward!' People run and shove in the darkness in the rear trench. They carry fresh ammunition to the front in sacks and boxes. The machine guns chatter so greatly and eat up so many cartridges that one must ceaselessly feed them new supplies. Again the phone rings. 'All available medical orderlies to come forward!' The communication trench is stuffed full of wounded and dead. The medical orderlies rush forward with an accomplished air and return bloody, like a butcher. The wounded that they carry back smell strongly of ammonium chloride, and men grope about by themselves, they could hardly see out of their eyes. This was because the Englishmen fire with gas shells out of which billow fumes that stun. [At this stage the British did not have gas shells; the Germans were victims of their own gas.]

The hours go by. Nobody counts them anymore. The battle does not want to end. The night has turned into hell. The telephone rings again, the fighters in the front urgently demand more, more and more hand grenades; then sand bags; then 'armoured shields, please send armoured shields'. Throughout the tenacious, grim man to man fighting of the Germans' and Englishmen's struggle for victory the pioneers filled sand bags, erected them for defence and erected armoured steel shields in to them. An enemy shell brazenly drops down so that even the well built, arduously constructed fortifications of sand bags and armoured shields were sprayed aside in a flaming cone. The dead are torn apart in all manner.

Out of the night people continually come out of the hell storm that rages about Hill 60 toward the rear trench. They are like singed cinders separated out of the fire of battle. Some of them drag themselves bleeding to the dressing station, but for some of them it is not the muscles of the body but the mind that begins to fail. Some have lost their speech and some have lost their minds and do something at the time which is utterly pointless. Others can no longer see or hear anything because of the noise, the continuous horrible crashing and rattle. The night goes on like this, it seems indefinite. Furstenau [the Regiment's commander] *writes the following in his diary: 'I am freezing, I wish it would become light. The darkness is horrible.'*

And it finally becomes day. All the horrors could not have broken German courage and bravery. English prisoners said three English Army Corps had been placed in the night against the 105th Regiment.

This statement is, of course, a gross exaggeration - it was more like three battalions against the 105th.

On the other hand, it is possible to get plenty of less emotionally involved views of things from the German perspective. The 127th Infantry Regiment, which describes much about the 'ordinary' aspect of the war, the daily routine and the peculiar problems that arose from the nature of the Hill 60 sector.

The 127th Regiment had been in the Argonne, beautiful wooded and hilly country not far from Verdun.

The German position ringing Ypres was like the edge of a bowl, with Ypres located at its deepest point. It lay only a few thousand metres distant. However above the parapet one could not see the city, at least in the regimental sector at Hill 60, as, unlike the Argonne where an occasional look over the top could be dared in quiet times, here the enemy was hellish and his marksmen were always at hand. However, if one moved to the stereo telescope of the Observation Post, then the charming sight of Ypres, white fire trenches and the triangular shape of Zillebeke Lake in the foreground were mysteriously gathered together in the glass.

Such a position lying upon the edge of the hill afforded insights into the rear areas; he probably also owned some high points, but most of them were in our hands. Naturally the fierce fighting on the German side occurred because under no circumstances could the enemy be allowed to seize the heights and, if at all possible, the aim was to throw the enemy off those heights they still possessed. Meanwhile the Englishman fought with tenacity for the opposite goal. The Anglo-Saxon's hard head and the Swabian's not so soft head butted against each other here. Because the English were not, up to now, successful in reaching their goal in open fighting, they attempted it by different means: namely through undermining the German positions and mine explosions. Thus Hill 60 was a part of the terrain that had already been blown up repeatedly by friend and foe. You had to be careful there. The German side drove a net of walking tunnels forward that were positioned so deep that the enemy could not easily go under them and thus under the German position.

KNOLL ROAD

THE SNOUT

BRITISH TRENCH

SAUBUCHT

STINKGRABEN

ZWARTELEEN

HILL 60

RAILWAY CUTTING

Willkommen in der Saubucht!

Stinkgraben

GERMAN AERIAL PHOTOGRAPH

Verbrandenmol

The Ravine

34

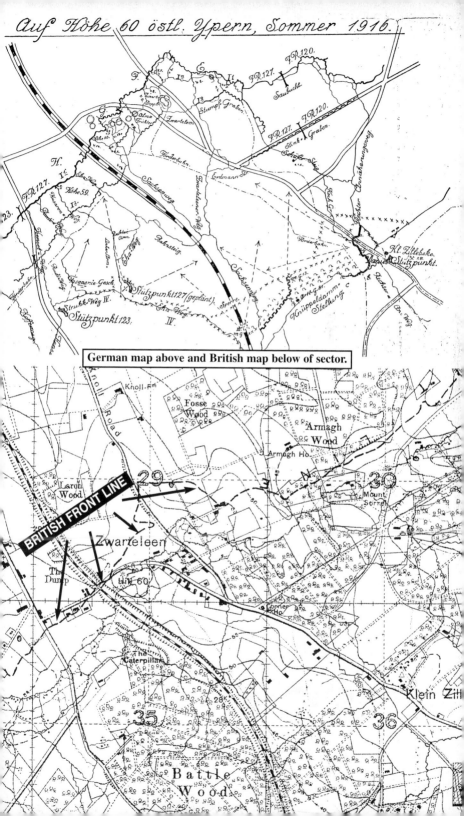

Auf Höhe 60 östl. Ypern, Sommer 1916.

German map above and British map below of sector.

BRITISH FRONT LINE

Large craters were formed and from the air the hill looked like a lunar landscape filled with craters. The struggle under the earth went on day and night. Whoever got in with their mine explosion first had won that particular battle. If one first heard the enemy working underground close to, then it meant that immediate action was required. The professional miner's expression was 'to blow in the enemy'. Detonators were quickly put in, and after a few minutes only a ray of fire shooting up out of the ground indicated the position where living persons had breathed underneath it. The occupation of the miners was infinitely dangerous and destroyed their nerves under these circumstances; and many of the men from the Regiment were called upon to work below the surface.

The construction of the position was completely different from the Argonne. The ground in Ypres lay only just above sea level whilst a large part consisted of sand and wetland, so there was no possibility of digging trenches in many positions. Instead they were created above ground by the use of thousands upon thousands of sandbags. This work (and it was the same for the enemy) required a great deal of effort. Under these circumstances it was easy for both sides to see their opponent's positions. The dugouts had to be made in part from concrete blocks above ground. When the ground had to be penetrated it called for careful, incessant drainage. An extensive rail network was built in order to bring the numerous trench stores forward. The consumption of planks, wire netting, beams, cement and gravel was enormous. In the night hours the platoons came to the still operable Ypres-Comines railway line with caution and brought all of the required materials to the unloading ramp.

The battle sector of the Regiment stretched via the aforementioned railway line, via Hill 60 and then off in a north eastern direction, moving over the remains of the village of Zwarteleen, only indicated by a few bricks, and then went into a small grove and then into a clearing, known as the Pig Sty. This is not a charming name (nor that of the nearby Stinkgraben), but was so christened because it was once a pig sty and because, during our advance, the enemy fired 'big pigs' into this little corner. The dugouts, in any case, were aptly named pig sties, especially when the marshy water came pouring in.

The enemy used very heavy calbre guns here, especially naval guns - in fact this was the first time we became acquainted with such weapons. His ball mines [toffee apple mortars, probably] were very effective. The numerous enemy rifle grenades used by him became disconcerting. The small amount of English activity until after about 10 am proved to be strange. It appeared that Tommy first bathed as well as had his breakfast first.

A similar, second, position was placed behind the forward most line, a short distance from there. Several hundred metres to the rear there followed a second defensive line, but was at the time only considered as an idea.

The Regiment remained in the sector until the end of July and took part in the attack against the Canadians against Double Hill 60. On 18 July a night time raid took

Captured (in the attack of 2 June 1917) Canadian prisoner in Tenbeielen.

a Canadian prisoner from whom it was firmly established that he was from the 16th Battalion in the 4th Canadian Division. In addition a day book which was kept up until 15 July was captured, along with rifles, side arms, pieces of equipment entrenching tools and hand grenades.

Part of the aim was to destroy English mine galleries with bundled charges, but this form of attack usually only caused superficial damage to the shafts, as can be seen in the chapter on mining.

The Regiment was glad to move away from Hill 60; but they might have been less glad if they knew what was to await them at Guillemont, on the Somme, where they arrived in August and stayed for three very bloody weeks.

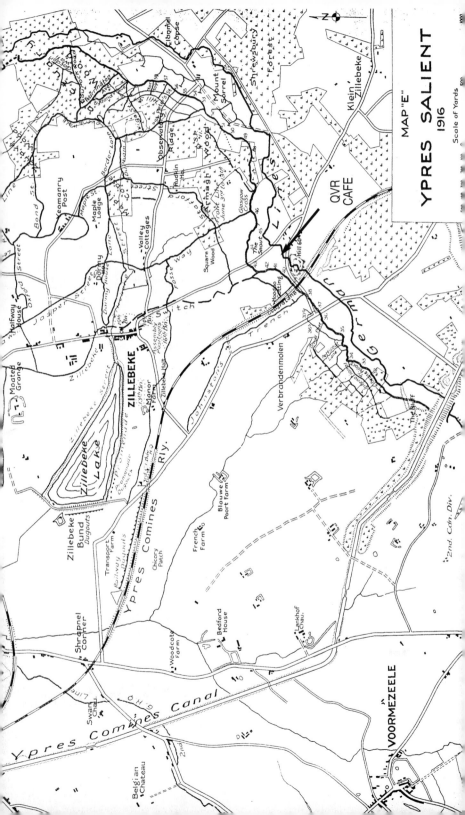

MAP "E"

YPRES SALIENT
1916

Scale of Yards

Chapter Five

THE BRITISH ON THE DEFENSIVE: EPISODES AT HILL 60, 1915 AND 1916.

To this sector came the 46th (North Midland) Division in July 1915, remaining there until the beginning of October, before they marched away to take part in the bloody actions around the Hohenzollern Redoubt later that month.

A Daily Mail correspondent described the trenches around Hill 60 in an article of August 1915:

The hill, which is of a low elevation, rising only some thirty feet above the surrounding country, is really nothing but a rising knoll of ground that forms the end of the Klein Zillebeke ridge. The German trenches run in a double tier along the crest and upper slope, while our trenches form an irregular line along the edge of the lower slope. The enemy is at the top of the hill, and we are a little way up the side of it. The whole face of the hill presents a picture of the wildest confusion. Everywhere are huge craters, results of mines exploded on the night of the British attack, torn and gaping sandbags are scattered in profusion, broken rifles, British and German, odds and ends of equipment of all kinds, smashed barbed wire, and a mass of other debris, lie in bewildering variety, down the hill side, the whole half hidden in the long grass that has sprung up between the trenches. The

A British position behind Hill 60. Note the extensive use of sandbags, but the position is vulnerable to a well-aimed shell.

1/6 South Staffordshire Regiment, photographed with one of their officers, soon after their arrival in France. The men are armed with the long rifle, and are wearing caps stiffened with wire. Later the wire was taken out as the stiff tops caught the light and were visible at a long distance.

latter twist and wind in an extraordinary way.

At one place I reached a spot but six yards from the enemy, and down this trench two barricades have been erected, one on our side and one on the German side. Between the two sides there is a short patch of ground shut in, on either side, by the crumbling walls of the old trench.

At one spot a railway bridge spans our position, and in the cutting beneath a large pool of stagnant water has collected. Beyond stretches the railway line, the rails torn and twisted, and partly covered with weeds growing between the sleepers. In a pool below the bridge are a number of ghastly relics, the exact nature of which is best left to the imagination. It is enough to say that dead men have been lying there for some months, and no man dare to approach to bring them out for burying.

It was a pouring afternoon when we went round, and the trenches were wet and slippery. The floor was covered with a thick layer of rich brown mud. The men sought cover as best they could, some huddled under rainproof sheets, and others crouched in dugouts.

The Staffordshire Brigade (137) held the trenches adjacent to the railway cutting.

The worst of the situation was probably due to the fact that the Battalion was occupying trenches only recently constructed, and adapted as fire trenches. they were sited more by necessity than by choice, and devoid of any amenity whatsoever, save that of being holes in which to avoid whizz-bangs. These seemed to come from a distance of about a hundred yard- whatever the exact range it was probably as short as it could be made in trench warfare. For six continuous days of appalling heat, tormented by drought and plague of flies, we were experiencing the results of being a close target for vicous enemy field-gunners, themselves comfortably ensconced and liberally supplied. Some consolation was afforded from time to time by the deafening reports of our own heavies, said to be naval-armour piercing, in the adjoining enemy's midst; but this pleasure was but illusory and short-lived, since the Germans never allowed their infantry to be much punished, without doubly and quickly punishing ours. To a detached strategist this may sound reasonable and interesting, but to us it was, to put it lightly, irksome.

Battalion HQ dugout of 1/6 South Staffs in Larch Wood. Note the chair!

One of the officer's of 6/South Staffs wrote in his first letter, after his first tour in the sector in which two officers and thirty five ORs were wounded and two killed,

> *I have nothing to write on and nowhere to write. This is just a deep, cramped trench and nothing more; no dugouts, no shade and nothing at all except an endless supply of large shells always arriving. I wonder if there is any limit to the discomforts of which life is capable? It looks as if it was going to rain tonight; that at any rate will lay the flies and provide me with a drop of something to wash in.*

> *I feel more cheerful about the situation after a wash in half a pint of water, procured from somewhere or other for his Company by the incomparable Billy Lewis. As a result of the shelling, my bit of trench has got cut off again from the Company's sector, and has become a separate command. We've got an excellent melon for lunch, which brightens things up a bit. But this is all rather a nerve-racking affair, and we shall be glad when the tour is over. Things come over so suddenly, and make such a noise when they arrive. Billy Lewis had a large one quite close to him this morning, as he was doing his rounds; but he profited by the depth of his communication trench, he tells me, and it all passed off nicely. (A*

Men of 1/6 S. Staffs Regiment, sleeping in a trench, Hill 60, August 1915.

Trench 47, Ypres 1915. Left to right, Private Foulkes, Corporal Kent, Sergeant Burdett, Sergeant Gibbons of the 4/Leicesters.

small but effective one arrived here, just at the word 'nicely'.) I suppose there will be two more or so, and then half an hour's peace again...There's the second, damn it; and here's the third, but not quite so near. You simply have to sit and wait for the devils, but the first is always the worst of the series. And here's a fourth, by way of postscript! I expect they will now go on doing this all day, because we put in a lot of work last night, and that always seems to try their temper. I suppose they are not as bad as a bullet, but there comes a time when you'd prefer the short sharp snap to this sudden bang in your very midst. And, hell take it, there's a fifth and a sixth!...It appears to be over now, for the moment, and the next incident is the arrival of the Brigadier - an outspoken soldier with a brusque manner which he probably doesn't mean, but as honest as they are made, and with little or none of the red-hat business about him. He evidently believed in sharing the risks we run. When he has soundly rated a man for taking a glimpse over the parapet, he climbs up and does it himself.

Early days out of the line were not better, either. There were nights when the weather was very bad. Then

even the men's ingeniously contrived and well constructed bivouacs afforded no protection against the water which crept in underneath, even if it failed to come through at the top. One officer reported,

'One's men are in worse plight even than oneself; but last night, when the limits of misery seemed to be reached in the drenching downpour, and the dismal groans (playfully

129

emphasised) were coming from the bivouacs, one fellow set us all laughing by giving the most remarkable and life-like imitation of a duck quacking as it happily took to its favourite element. No jest was ever found more timely or better received. The place was a sheet of water, and most of us were well in it! And as if life was not hard enough already, they fetched us up at 4.30 am to come and dig.'

Not the least evil of these conditions was the endless way we had to march to and from the trenches - to and from the fatigues. A testimonial is due to our late Quartermaster for the faithful provision of abundant tea at half-way; though how we can ever have drunk that appalling sweetened syrup and enjoyed it, now passes comprehension.

As far as 6/South Staffs were concerned, this tour in this sector was a terrible one, a continuous grinding away of daily trench wastage, in miserable trenches, poor rest areas, under the threat of being blasted skywards by mines and very vulnerable to German artillery fire, which persisted for infrequent intervals daily - and nightly.

Then there was the depression of one of those quiet-time officer casualties, always striking, at the instant, more poignantly. The Colonel's diary records the event.

During the night [of 24/25 September] *the Brigadier* [Feetham] *called and inquired if a patrol had been sent out from Trench 37, and asked that it should be made an officer's patrol. Sankey was commanding the Company, Billy Lewis being on leave, and he sent Nelson, a new officer, out. Apparently Sankey*

A periscopic rifle being demonstrated in the Hill 60 area, 1915.

got anxious, as Nelson did not immediately return, and took a look over the parapet. He was shot through the head and brought down to Lane's dugout in so hopeless a condition that obviously nothing could be done. He died at 4.30 am. Poor boy! 'Sydney John', as he was affectionately called by the other officers, was a sound, quiet boy, with plenty of ability which did not at once appear on the surface; extremely zealous and dependable, always anxious to be working. Had seen much of him this last week in 37, and he was full of good ideas. The tragedy of it is that he was going home in a week or two to be married, and had applied for a special ten days' leave for the purpose. He joined the battalion about four years ago. We buried him in Larch Wood in the afternoon.

He is buried in Larch Wood cemetery, in I L5; he was aged 25.

The sad tale of Captain Sankey reflects a general feeling that the old battalion was dying - that it was undergoing a transformation as more and more of its originals died off; this feeling is also reflected in other battalion histories. Yet an ability to make the most of everything, and where possible to see the funny side of anything, remained.

Lieutenant-Colonel Waterhouse's diary, a wonderful source of information, to be cut short by his serious wounding on 8 October, has a delightful last reference to the area.

A very senior officer of the Staff concluded his address of farewell to the Battalion in the following words, which have never been forgotten:

'...And I shall watch the future career of the 6/South Staffs with the greatest interest and sympathy. Where's my car?'

To the left of 6/South Staffs and 5/North Staffs were the Territorials of the Leicestershire Regiment. Their time in the Hill 60 sector started quietly enough.

From July 13th to the 19th the battalion remained comfortably in the railway dugouts [ie in the area near the present day cemetery of that name] *basking in the sunshine and complacently watching Ypres being shelled during the day and uncomplainingly carrying out fatigues at night. So far so good.*

See map page 124

On the 18th, however, there was a tragedy. Lieutenant FN Tarr was killed. You had to know Frank Tarr and to be in the battalion to realise what that meant; no words can ever explain.

He was killed by a splinter from a 'krump' whilst he was visiting the Zillebeke Lake dugouts. The Boche was industriously shelling a field cooker which stood out under a hedge close by, and Tarr put his head out of a dugout to tell some men to keep under cover when a splinter hit him in the face. If it had been any other part of his body it would have caused only the slightest of wounds, a mere scratch, but that only made it more tragic. This happened in the afternoon.

That night, surrounded by his friends, he was buried not very far from where he had fallen [Railway Dugouts, Transport Farm: I E.8] *and the Brigade Chaplain read the burial service. It was a sad night for everybody, for Frank Tarr was the most attractive*

131

Back row, left to right: **2/Lt G E F Russel, 2/Lt J F Johnson, 2/Lt W N Dunn, Lt G A Brogden,** RAMC, **2/Lt F M White**
Second row from back, left to right: **2/Lt M B Douglas, 2/Lt H F Papprill, Lt J G Abell, Lt F N Tarr, Lt W B Jarvis**
Lt G J Harvey, Lt A Silver, 2/Lt H C Brice, Lt F S Parr, Lt & QM A E Ball. *Third row from back, left to right:* **Cap**
R A Faire, Capt B F Newill, Capt A C Cooper, Maj L V Wykes, Lt-Col W A Harrison, Capt & Adjt R S Dyer-Benne
Capt T P Fielding-Johnson, Capt J C Baines, Capt H Haylock. *Front row, left to right:* **Lt T Whittingham, 2/Lt A C**
Clarke, 2/Lt R C Harvey, 2/Lt L Forsell.

> *personality in the battalion, young [he was 27], good looking,*
> *full of charm, with an eye that always had a twinkle in it, a born*
> *leader, yet the kindest person possible, a Rugger international,*
> *the idol of the machine gun section, which he commanded before*
> *he became adjutant.*
>
> *Everybody was heart-broken, for everybody would miss him;*
> *they would not look upon his like again.*
>
> *And so, as the darkness fell, they buried him by stealth, with*
> *silent salutes and stifled tears. And the transport officer, who had*
> *played David to his Jonathan, caused a large white cross of*
> *wood to be made, a larger cross than any which stood around,*
> *that all who passed might see and remember a great three-*
> *quarter and a greater gentleman.*

The regimental history of 1/4th Leicesters is anecdotal in nature which, besides being different, highlights the gentler and more humorous aspects of a unit's history in wartime. One of the more poignant vignettes relates to a young soldier.

> *One night near the Verbranden Molen a man was hit*
> *belonging to a fatigue party carrying timber for mining; he was*
> *sent to a medical aid-post nearby, and when the fatigue was over*
> *the officer in charge sent on the party and called to see how the*
> *man was. As it was not safe to walk alone he selected a youngster*
> *out of the party to accompany him. This boy was a stocky little*

fellow who spent most of his time hanging over the parapet when his section commander was not looking; he was one of the rapid fire artists and the word fear was not in his vocabulary.

While the two were walking back to the railway dugouts the officer for some reason or other asked the boy his age.

'Unofficial or official, sir,' came the prompt reply.

'Unofficial, of course,,' said the officer.

'Well, sir, you promise you won't get me into trouble if I tell you?'

'Not likely, and you need not think I shall have you sent home if you are under age.'

'I'm just sixteen,' hissed the happy young warrior through his teeth. He always tried to look as bellicose as possible, and longed for the day when he would be able to grow a moustache like his company sergeant-major.

'Why did you join up so young?'

'Because all the other boys in the street were joining, and I wasn't going to be left behind.'

Just sixteen, and already under fire for six months!

The sequel happened a few days later.

The boy went down to the dressing station one morning with a stretcher party carrying a wounded NCO. On the way back through Armagh Wood they were caught by some shrapnel, and the boy was mortally wounded. In his agony he cried and called for his mother, and shortly afterwards he died.

He was a typical example of that comparatively rare species, 'the born fighting man,' a d'Artagnan in miniature. He enjoyed danger, he laughed at hardship, he loved fighting. Only a year or two previously he was playing at soldiers and Red Indians, but now here was the real thing all free, gratis and for nothing, and wasn't it fun! Real rifles and bayonets, real bombs and, alas, real shrapnel.

The Leicesters position was to the left of Hill 60, for the most part beyond Knoll Road. Indeed the 4/Leicesters left their mark on the trench maps in the form of Fosse Way; and also in the name given to the Canadian Memorial just beyond Sanctuary Wood Cemetery and the Museum there. Mount Sorrel was not a name that existed in this part of Belgium; the small eminence gained its title from the Leicestershire village where the CO of 4/Leicesters came from - Mountsorrel, not far from Loughborough. Indeed, the Canadian memorial is not situated on this point on the trench map in any case; it is on Hill 62.

A listening post ten yards from the German trenches on Hill 60.

The battalion had an increasingly difficult time in the sector as time passed by. Entries in the War Diary in September indicate this in a somewhat terse fashion:

49 and 50 trenches whizz-banged during the afternoon. 48 trench sausaged. Enemy shelled communication trenches 47S and 42A.

These simple phrases meant an uneasy life and perhaps an uncomfortable death. At this period the enemy 'crumped' our trenches very heavily and the sandbag barricades had to be built up again by night, which entailed extra fatigue parties and a lot of very hard work. The Railway Dugouts were also shelled, and the Boche put one large shell into the pond [this is the farm pond by transport farm, still there]*, much to the disgust of the local anglers.*

But though the Germans were making themselves thoroughly disagreeable, there was one thing with which they could not interfere, and that was the evening sunset. And what sunsets they were; fiery, blood-red, full of majesty, full of foreboding. Just as the men in the trenches were 'standing-to' the sun was going down behind the ruins of the Cloth Hall like some gigantic pigeon-blood ruby, and the heavens were filled with all manner of redness, pink, scarlet, vermilion, couleur de rose. And sentimental Private Atkins cleaning his rifle in 47 (the international trench, ten yards from the Germans) gazed with admiration mingled with solemn wonder; it was such a magnificent sight, but it was so awfully red, so very much like blood.

The two Leicesters battalions were not directly involved in the action at Bellewaarde on 25 September, to their left; but they were part of a decoy plan, which involved the burning of straw along their parapets. This was highly effective, where it worked, drawing heavy artillery fire on the 5th Leicesters; elsewhere the straw was too wet to burn![1]

The next major excitement on Hill 60 occurred in June 1916; but once again, the main fight was to the left, and the participants this time were men of the Canadian Corps.

The 16th Battalion (Canadian Scottish) CEF

The Germans, in order to hamper operations on the Somme, carried out a limited attack against the Canadian 3rd Division between Maple Copse and Hooge on 2 June 1916. This was at first very successful, and drove the Canadians back some distance, inflicting quite heavy casualties. However, on 13 June 1916 the Germans were themselves turfed out of their positions almost all the way along the line, except that opposite Hooge the British line was withdrawn permanently to a more defendable location some several hundred yards to the west of its former location. The 16th Battalion (along with the 13th in support) was an active participant in restoring the line on the Canadian right.

With the battle over, a long period of resting, absorbing drafts and reorganisation followed; then the 16th was moved to the Hill 60 sector on 16 July. This battalion is blessed with one of the finest regimental histories ever published, not least in its comprehensive series of appendices which run for over five hundred pages.[2] Its time of seven weeks serving in the Hill 60/Mount Sorrel sectors produced 495 casualties, 97 of which were fatal. Its last stint ran from 25 June to 8 August, a period in which one officer and thirty men were killed.

It would be fair to say that the 16th Battalion did not much like the Hill 60 sector; indeed the battalion had earned the ire of higher authority when it lost a prisoner to the Germans in a raid on the Canadian lines which was covered by one of those great trench-mortar bombardments of which the Germans were such experts.

On 1 August the battalion returned to Hill 60,

> to complete the sum of its experience in that sector by taking part in one of the mining enterprises which, more than any other form of activity, made the name of Hill 60 known far and wide on the British front. The trenches in this sector, at the widest, were little more than fifty yards apart.

It was during this last tour here that the mining officers decided that something had to be done about advanced German saps that threatened some of the British mines; a surgical operation was required to remove these without damaging the complex network of British mines, which existed on at least three different levels in this sector in a very tight area.

After calculations it was agreed that the task could best be accomplished by two camouflets - small mines which explode downwards. They usually disturbed the surface of the earth very little; but in this instance, as the charge was placed at a shallow depth and was of considerable strength, it was expected two craters would be formed, partly in the enemy's lines and partly in No Man's Land.

The problem was that the ground conditions were so difficult to predict that it was possible that a miscalculation could cause the firer as many problems as the intended recipient of the blow. These possibilities were not explained to the troops who had to engage in these undertakings - their imagination was probably boggling enough as it was without adding to the burden.

The blow would take place at 10 pm on 3 August; the 16th would provide the men to occupy and consolidate the craters. This included ten bombers, with another ten on stand-by; a digging party of twenty men; a consolidating party of six men with filled sandbags with ten

German hand-grenades with handles for carrying and slinging were very effective for fighting at close quarters. Here they can can be seen watching through the loopholes for opportunities to throw.

more on standby; an expert party of nine men from Battalion and Brigade to do the wiring, with another nine on stand by; whilst a covering party was to try and hold the enemy trench in front of 39 and 40 whilst the consolidation was completed. See map page 124

At zero hour the charge was fixed; the earth was tossed into the air, carrying with it all the gruesome wreckage which encumbered No Man's Land: the road, which there passed between the lines, went up in 'chunks as big as pianos'; the artillery and the machine guns took their part according to the plan. But unfortunately the unforeseen error had crept in. The explosion blew back unduly, wrecking the Canadian trenches and partially burying the bombing party and reserves. Some were crushed to death and all were shaken.

When the remnants of the party, in particular the bombers, who were to secure the flanks of the crater on the enemy side, rushed forward they expected to find themselves in what had been the enemy's front line. Instead they found themselves looking at a German trench more or less untouched, as the mine had exploded short; obviously there was no question of penetrating the German line, rather it was now a case of fending off German attacks until the British side of the crater could be consolidated.

The cost was heavy - possibly worthwhile if the mining objective of destroying the German saps was achieved. The fatal casualties of this raid are buried in a long row, along with others from the battalion during its tours, in Larch Wood Cemetery in IV G.

Indeed, the fight for the crater went on right up to the relief of the Battalion. This set-to resulted in the death of Lieutenant John Ellis, the Intelligence Officer - recently commissioned (in June) from the ranks. The Germans were trying to outflank a wiring party; the Battalion bombers went out to try and cut the

Germans off. This resulted in a shower of German 'potato masher' grenades landing amongst the me of the 16th. Lieutenant Ellis, as he was about to fling a Mills grenade, was wounded - fatally as it proved - by a splinter from one of these bombs. He had the presence of mind to keep his finger on the lever of the bomb and pass it to Lieutenant Lyons, who threw it at the moment when another German bomb landed close to Ellis's head. Lyons kicked this missile away, but it exploded, rendering him unconscious and wounding him in the leg. The Germans were driven off.

Lieutenant Ellis is buried at Hazebrouk Communal Cemetery; there was a Casualty Clearing Station at this important railhead town, and he had made it back thus far from the line.

13th Battalion (Royal Highlanders of Canada) CEF

On 14 July 1916 the 13th moved into the line on the south side of the cutting, with the 16th to their left, opposite Hill 60. When they came into the line the history describes the trenches as being 'in a very fair condition'. Indeed, behind the front line it was quite possible to move about in the open because of the protection of the ' abundant foliage'.

All was to be unsettled by a severe trench bombardment opened up on the Hill 60 sector at 8 pm on 18 July, in particular across the railway cutting and the front of the 13th.

Retaliation started at once, but the advantage was all with the Germans. The Stokes gun crews worked courageously, but were literally snowed under. Unfortunately, too, one of the supporting 60-pounder Trench Mortar Batteries went wrong at this time and crashed a series of bombs into the Highlanders' trenches.

The majority of the men on the left, ie at the railway cutting, and where the bombing was least severe, were withdrawn and the position held by a bombing squad. In the centre the bombing was most severe. Indeed the company commander had a narrow escape, when his life was saved

> by the vigilance of a runner, Private Dunn, who saw the torpedo coming and gave the Captain a warning which enabled him to escape.

The Germans then pushed forward several attacks.

> Of these, the main one was directed against the point where the right of the 16th and the left of the 13th rested on the railway cutting. One small party entered a trench from which the 16th had been withdrawn and started to cross the stone arch [ie the

138

bridge] *over the cutting. The members of this party were revealed
by the light of a flare and were seen to be wearing flat caps with
Red Cross brassards. Challenged by Lance Corporal Johnson, a
Russian in the 13th ranks, they made some guttural answer to
which Johnson, suspecting a trick, replied with a bomb. The
Germans promptly returned the compliment, whereupon the
Lance Corporal and his party drove them back across the bridge*
[ie to the Hill 60 side], *their retreat being hastened by a machine
gun which opened on them from a distance.*

The front line was rapidly remanned by the Canadians and thereby they
threw back the attack against Trench 37 S, which was immediately
adjoining the cutting.

Another incident on Hill 60, another fifteen men or so killed on the
Canadian side - nothing unusual in the so-called 'quiet time' at Hill
60.[3]

1. The sources for this section come from the Regimental histories of 6th South Staffordshire
Regiment, *The History of the 5th North Staffordshire Regiment, The Fifth Leicestershire* and
Footprints of the 1/4th Leicestershire Regiment.
2. *History of the 16th Battalion (The Canadian Scottish)* CEF, HM Urquhart, DSO MC ADC.
Macmillan Co of Canada, 1932.
3. *The 13th Battalion Royal Highlanders of Canada 1914 - 1919*, ed and compiled by RC
Featherstonhaugh. By the Regiment 1925.

EPILOGUE: 1918

This is a short chapter - not because the events of 1918 were
insignificant, but because that which made Hill 60 so memorable
happened in the years preceding it.

Hill 60 was abandoned, in a planned withdrawal, on 15th April 1918
by the 21st Division, which withdrew to a line west of Zillebeke Lake.
My grandfather was a member of 110 Brigade, and spent some days in
occupation of Railway Dugouts. His division had been in the fighting
on the Somme, at Epehy, here, at the Lys, and was to be again the
victim of a German offensive on the Aisne in the next month.

On 28 September the 35th Division, with the 14th on its right just
north of the Bluff, swept through the old Hill 60 positions and on
almost to Zandvoorde. Hill 60 does not even rate a mention in the
Official History accounts of the German and Anglo-Belgian offensives
of 1918; it comes down to being only a breathing point for two days in
that tumultuous and significant year.

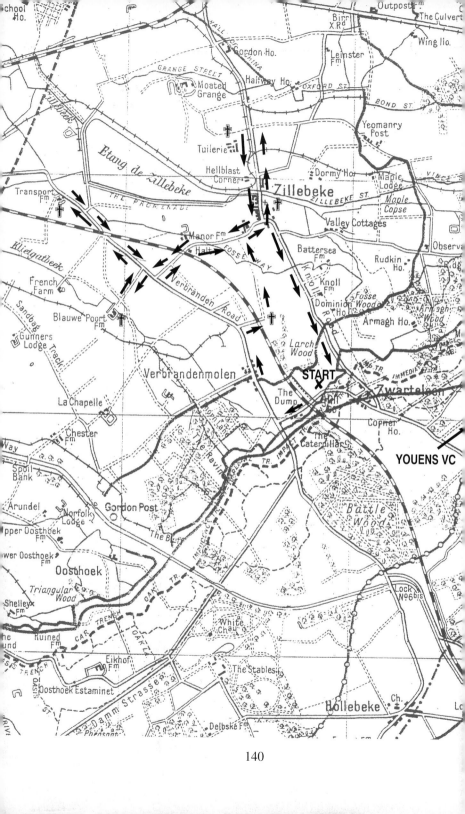

Chapter Six

THE TOUR

This tour can be done by a series of hops in a car or as a long walk. The preference would be for the latter, because it will enable the visitor to Hill 60 to walk the ground that many of the men who fought here did, as well as being better able to observe the topographical features, the shallow valleys and the views that help to inform. On a personal note, I have always found being in the place where something happened as of great importance and significance to me; time spent walking these now busy roads, and through villages which have not only been rebuilt but also sizeably expanded still seems to me to bring closer those men and events of over eighty years ago. The walk will take a long morning and there are only limited watering facilities. A way round this might well be to base yourself at the car park by the Queen Victoria's Rifles café, do the distance walking first and then leave Hill 60 itself until last; or cover Hill 60 first and then do the walking, taking the opportunity to have a drink and a lunch break in the interval.

It is possible to eat your lunch at the tables in the café, but you need to buy the necessary elements first; there is a small supermarket just beyond the café, towards the Klein Zillebeke road, but it might be best to stock up in Ypres first. This is also your chance to look around the somewhat chaotic display of artefacts in the museum beyond the bar. They might not be presented in a high tech way, but there is something almost more real about them as a consequence. The café and the museum are open daily from about 10 am to 7 pm, though this can be somewhat erratic.

Your car should be parked in the space available alongside the QVR café; please take rudimentary security precautions, such as putting obvious

Hill 60 and surrounding area.

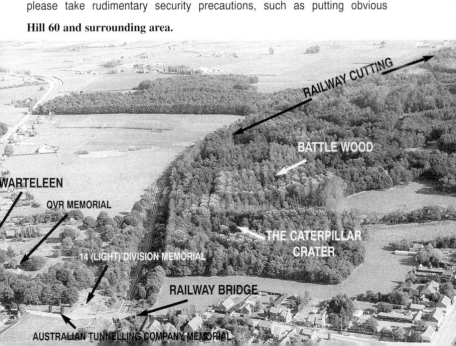

Above: **Part of the display in the museum in the QVR café.**
Left: **A trench mortar outside the café.**

valuables in the boot. I have not heard of any cases of theft from cars in Belgium (they seem to be more prevalent on the Somme), but it would be as wise to be cautious.

Hill 60

Opposite the café there is a small gate leading into the preserved area around Hill 60. Enter through this, ensuring that the gate does shut behind you, or else the sheep might decide to explore!

Up the slope of the hill is the Queen Victoria's Rifles memorial. It is not in the position that one might have expected; most of their fighting was off, further to the right. Its location is probably a matter of convenience, as it is on the highest spot and the ground is likely to be more stable here. In any case, the June 1917 mine would have removed the ground over which the men of this battalion fought in 1915. Looking along parallel to the road

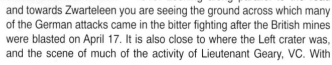

The rebuilt QVR Memorial.

and towards Zwarteleen you are seeing the ground across which many of the German attacks came in the bitter fighting after the British mines were blasted on April 17. It is also close to where the Left crater was, and the scene of much of the activity of Lieutenant Geary, VC. With

Exploring German trenches on
Hill 60 in the interwar years.

your back to the memorial, looking the way which you came, and then to the half right, to the bottom right of the enclosure, is the site of the deep shell holes. On the café side of the road, more or less opposite a small building with a pointed roof (which is a small shrine) was where Dwyer won his VC.

The QVR memorial had a rather more magnificent approach before the Second World War and, of course, there were trenches and dugouts and underground shelters on both the British and the German side of the lines open to the public. The memorial was one of the very few memorials or cemeteries that were destroyed by the occupying German forces; it is said that this was done because it made reference to the first use of gas. The new memorial is a smaller, but nevertheless impressive, version of the original.

Continue walking to the south east (ie more or less straight ahead if you leave the memorial to your left). Almost immediately you will see a memorial plaque to one John Oliff, a veteran of the Second World War, whose ashes were scattered here in 1987. Proceed past this, and the various scattered remnants of concrete lying about and shortly before coming to a complete bunker you will be more or less on the advanced position which was occupied by Lieutenant Roupell VC and his men.

Not far from this you will see the famous Hill 60 bunker, which is on the forward, south eastern slope of the hill. Peter Oldham, in his book *Pill Boxes on the Western Front*, explains its complicated history:

> After the mine exploded on the morning of 7 June the Germans of the 20th Division in the bunkers and pill boxes were not in a condition to offer much resistance, and infantrymen of the Prince of Wales' Own West Yorkshires cleared the bunkers which had not been buried or destroyed. The British held the hill through the summer of 1917 and into the spring of 1918. In January and February, 1918, Hill 60, now on the corps defence line, was held by men of the 4th Australian Division. The 4th Field Company

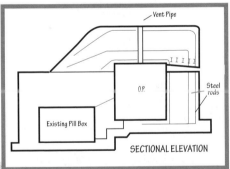

SECTIONAL ELEVATION

The June 7 1917 crater.

Australian Engineers, under Major J H Jolly, designed and built a pill box looking eastwards on top of an existing German bunker. An Australian machine-gun post was also sited in another pill box, the remains of which are 200 yards away. The position was given up to the Germans on the night of 15-16 April, 1918, with the British retiring to a line 400 yards to the west.

Proceed to the southernmost edge of the park; the woodland in the distance before you, on this side of the railway line, marks the approximate limit of the 23rd Division advance on 7 June 1917. The large expanse of wood on the other side of the railway line is Battle Wood.

Work your way towards the railway cutting and stroll back towards the road, but keeping close to the cutting. There are more scattered remnants of crater lying around. There then comes a large dip in the ground, which is the result of the Hill 60 mine of 7 June. It is not as impressive as many mine craters elsewhere, most memorably Lochnagar Crater on the Somme, but it is unusual for the Salient in that it is empty of water. Shortly after one enters this dip the German line from the Caterpillar side came across to the Hill 60 position. To the right is where the smallest of the April 1915 craters were fired (of which there is, of course, no trace, as it was obliterated in 1917) and where Lieutenant Wooley did much of the work that earned him his VC

At the end of the crater area a well defined path becomes apparent, and you are now coming into the British sector, just before the gate, and Trench 38, which was rather more forward of the line of the British position overall.

Leave the park and examine the stone plaque which in a number of succinct sentences outlines what happened on Hill 60 during the war. To the left is the memorial to the 1st Australian Tunnelling Company, one of the very few commemorations of the work of the tunnellers anywhere on the Western Front. The inscription is a little misleading, as it implies the company worked this particular sector from 1915-1918; they did not. They were here from November 1916 to the firing of the mines. It replaces a memorial erected immediately after the war; it has an added poignancy in that the inscription is scarred by bullet holes from the next great conflict.

See pag

1st Australian Tunnelling Co. memorial. The plaque is scarred with bullet holes from the Second World War.

Nearby there is a car park, along the top of which ran Trench 38. At the head of this space is the memorial to the 14th (Light) Division. This was moved to this site from Railway Wood in 1978; this was because the memorial was in danger of severe structural damage due to subsidence in its old location. Rectifying that sort of thing is extremely expensive, as has recently been shown by the restoration of the 47th (London) Division Memorial in High Wood, on the Somme, which was threatened by a similar fate. Perhaps if the great interest in the Great War was as clear then as it is now it might have been left where it was. However, the removal is not as irrelevant as it might seem, for the 14th fought alongside the 35th Division in the Advance to Victory and captured the area of the Bluff.

I would urge you not to rush through Hill 60; take your time and ponder. Choose your moment - come here early in the morning or as the afternoon turns to evening. It is a quiet and undisturbed spot, which lends itself to Remembrance. It is, quite likely, the most hard fought-over piece of ground in the fiercely disputed Immortal Salient. Underneath the ground there must lie the remains of many hundreds of men,

14th (Light)
Division
Memorial

killed above and below it. They are most worthy of our consideration, these young men of both sides who were called, willing or not, to fight for their countries: Germans, Frenchmen (all too often neglected) and British.

Walk back a bit now, towards the café. Look towards Ypres. What a view the Germans had over the British lines; because the trees obscure matters further back, one does not get the full benefit of what they saw from five or ten metres higher up. The achievement of the British army in holding this line - and indeed the line around the Salient - was considerable. You also need to see this in the context of the decision to hold the Salient at all: why? The answer lies in the fact that the British were fighting in someone else's country: territory to the British might not matter, but it did to the Belgians, where Ypres, Furnes (Veurne) and Poperinge were the only places of significance not behind German lines. The canal might have been a more obvious defence line, but the Salient carried enormous emotive power. The British and French armies had fought an amazing action to bring the Germans to a standstill here in November 1914 and it most certainly could not lightly be relinquished.

Return back to the car park near the cutting, and note by its edge, alongside the depths of the cutting and the railway bridge, is a memorial to two Belgians

THE DUMP   YPRES   LARCH WOOD CEMETERY

From the railway bridge looking back over the British lines towards Ypres.

killed here in October 1944.

Walk across the railway bridge, and find a safe place to stop. Look along the line, with Hill 60 on your left and the Caterpillar on your right. Within a hundred yards or so was the German barricade and crossing of the railway line. On the

right is Battle Wood and the site of the Caterpillar. Prior to the Great War this area was not so heavily wooded, and the Caterpillar was relatively bare. Battle Wood has extended towards the north west and the water-filled crater is now fifty yards or so within its boundaries. Please note that this is a private wood and that the field between the road and the wood is also privately worked land. Do not just wander in, and I gather that visitors are not particularly welcome, although I have made no attempt myself to enter or to seek permission so to do. Running from the right of the bridge was Trench 37, and it was along here at a variety of suitable firing positions that the QVR machine gun caused considerable havoc amongst the German counter-attackers on 17 April 1915 and subsequently.

Cross the road and look down the British side of the railway cutting. On your left the tree covered mound is the Dump, and it was here that the British had their artillery observers.

A dugout of the 105th Howitzer Battery, 4th Brigade, Australian Field Artillery, near Hill 60 during the Third Battle of Ypres, 27 August 1917.

View from Caterpillar side of the railway bridge towards Hill 60.

Larch Wood has now, unfortunately, gone, but in the distance, close to the line, a white War Graves cross of sacrifice might just be made out. The fact that it is almost hidden in a dip in the ground goes some way to explaining why this area was relatively safe for the British, as it was beyond observed German fire; but it was pretty good odds that they would hit something if they fired down there!

Some distance before this there were British dugouts carved into the cutting which provided relative security; and, of course, there was the British barricade across the line.

Finally, continue walking over the bridge for maybe a hundred yards or so and then look back over the bridge and across the field before Battle Wood and get a feel for the prominence of Hill 60, this artificial heap of earth that survived the tens of thousands of pounds of explosives piled underneath it, shattered, altered but still there.

At this point you might want to return to your car and continue the tour on four wheels.

Behind Hill 60

The more hardy should continue walking until they come to a T junction and turn right. After about four hundred yards they will pass through the hamlet of Verbranden Molen. The mill used to stand on this side of the road that goes off to the left, which leads towards the Ravine and the canal. This part of the line will be covered in a later book in the series on the Bluff. From here Verbranden Road (its name during the war) gradually falls away, sitting on a small spur with

Larch Wood Cemetery

AUSTRALIAN 1st TUNNELLING
COMPANY MEMORIAL

small, hardly noticeable valleys forming on either side. British troops approaching Hill 60 either came across from billeting villages such as Reninghelst and came via Bedford House, the railway embankment and Johnson's Walk, a trench to the right of the railway, or from Shrapnel Corner, Railway Dugouts Zillebeke Lake/Zillebeke Halt and along the railway to Larch Wood.

After another three hundred yards or so you will come to the turning to Larch Wood cemetery; for those driving, you should be warned that it is on the bend

Molen Dump near Hill 60, where ammunition was concealed from German airmen and gunners.

of a road and along a track. In anything much wetter than a drought, it is practically impossible to turn around at the cemetery, so if you have any doubts about your reversing, you might be advised to park up and walk. Do not be tempted to try reversing in the fields - it is very boggy!

This track and crossing existed during the war. Be warned that the crossing is a simple look left and right arrangement - there are no barriers or warning lights. Also be warned that rail traffic is relatively frequent; in a half hour visit to the cemetery I saw two trains go by, and that was on a Saturday.

Before going up the cemetery path look sharp left, almost along the continuation of the approach track and see the squat tower of Zillebeke church. To its left you might catch a glimpse of Zillebeke Lake, an artificial stretch of water that for many years provided the water supply for Ypres. However in more recent years the authorities have constructed a new reservoir in the ground to the east of the Lille Gate in the marshy ground between the town and Verbranden Road.

Now look ahead of you and note the definite dip in the ground between here and Knoll Road. Out there was trench 42A, and to the south east was where some Germans managed to make their way through the disorganised British lines on 5 May and cause considerable disruption and casualties, including Lieutenant-Colonel Scott of the Cheshires, now buried in Zillebeke Churchyard.

Walk up the approach path to this beautifully sited cemetery. It was made at the north end of the wood, starting in April 1915, and was first used by 1/Dorsets. It was then extensively used by 46th (North Midland) Division and by a number of other units, although most bodies were removed, where practicable, to Railway Dugouts, further to the rear. A number of burials made here and in its vicinity, were lost in subsequent fighting or the marker was destroyed. There are just under 800 men buried here, of whom 321 are unidentified. After the war 245 bodies were brought in from isolated graves around about or from further afield, such as Bruges. Amongst those brought here was Lieutenant John Eden, the elder brother by some years of Sir Anthony Eden, later Lord Avon, the British Prime Minister during the Suez Crisis. Anthony Eden himself served in the Great War with some distinction; he does not seem to have been particularly close to his much older brother. Their father, who was much affected by the loss of his eldest son, died in 1915. John Eden, with three others, was brought in from America Cross Roads German Cemetery, and was killed on 17 October 1914 in the beginning stages of First Ypres. He was serving with the XIIth Royal Lancers and is buried in IV.D.6.

Also buried here in a line are men of the 16th Battalion CEF, including a number of those killed in the mine blast and subsequent fighting of 4 August 1916.

During the war extensive tunnels and shelters were constructed here (as also, for example, at Tor Top, where the Hill 62 Canadian Memorial now stands). Edmund Blunden, in his classic book, Undertones of War, described the area towards the end of 1917.

> *Larch Wood Tunnels were a magnificent work. The passages excelled in height and width and air supply. At this time they were principally in use as a medical headquarters, and once inside them it certainly seemed that safety and calm were assured. But outside people were being killed from time to time.*
>
> *A strange scene was to be viewed from the southward outlets of this tunnel – the deep old railway cutting past Hill 60, it was a dark canal now, the banks of which were shattered and the timbers tossed aside by*

Zillebeke churchyard, also known as the Aristocrats Cemetery. Overleaf, details of some of those buried here.

Lieutenant Henry Bligh Fortescue Parnell, 5th Baron Congleton
2 Battalion Grenadier Guards

He was the first member of the House of Peers to be killed in World War One; he suceeded his father as Baron in 1906. Lieutenant Lord Congleton was the eldest son of Major General Lord Congleton, C.B. and was born 6 September, 1890. He was educated at Eton and New College, Oxford and joined the Grenadier Guards as a University candidate in 1912. He was promoted Lieutenant in March 1913. He was a keen sportsman and traveller and he had hoped to go on an Antarctic expedition, which the war cancelled. He wrote articles on sporting subjects for magazines under the pseudonym, 'Con'. Lord Congleton was mentioned in Sir John French's Despatch on 14 January, 1915, for gallant conduct and skilful handling of his platoon against tremendous odds on 6 November, 1914, thereby saving the British line at that point. He was killed four days later in the action on 10 November, 1914.

Second Lieutenant Baron Alexis De Gunzburg
11 Hussars (Prince Albert's Own)

He received his commission in September, 1914 and became attached to the Royal Horse Guards, 7 Cavalry Brigade, as interpreter. Baron De Gunzburg, who was Russian by birth and educated at Eton, was naturalised in order to enlist in the British Army on the outbreak of war. His regiment went into the thick of the fighting in October 1914. He was killed 6 November and at the time was with the Life Guards. He had been sent along with three other officers to bring up the Royal Horse Guards to support an attack at Zillebeke. They were on foot and had to run across an open field for some 200 yards when on the way back, he was shot. His mother, Baroness De Gunzburg received a telegram from the King and Queen expressing their sympathy, and adding: "His Majesty has learnt how gallantly Baron De Gunzburg fought with his comrades of the Royal Horse Guards, although his duties as interpreter did not necessitate his presence in the firing line."

Major Lord Bernard Charles Gordon-Lennox
2 Battalion Grenadier Guards

He was the third son of the seventh Duke of Richmond and Gordon, K.G. He was born in London in May 1878 and educated at Eton College and Sandhurst, from which he joined the Grenadier Guards in 1898. He took part in the Boer War and the operations carried out in the Orange Free State, including actions at Poplar Grove and Driefontein, for which he received the Queen's medal with two clasps. From 1904-06 he was seconded for service with the Chinese Regiment at Wei-hai-Wei. He was promoted Captain in 1909 and became the Assistant Military Secretary to the then General Officer Commanding-in-Chief, Northern Command. For his services in the war he was mentioned in the supplement to Sir John French's Despatch 14 January, 1915. He was killed in action at Zillebeke 10 November, 1914. In 1907 Lord Bernard Gordon-Lennox married Evelyn, second daughter of the first Lord Loch, and left two sons.

Lieutenant Colonel Gordon Chesney Wilson, M.V.O.
Commanding The Royal Horse Guards

He was killed in action 6 November, 1914. He was the eldest son of Sir Samuel Wilson, M.P. and was born 3 August, 1865. He joined the Royal Horse Guards from the Militia and reached the rank of captain in 1894. He took part in the Boer War during which he was on the Staff as A.D.C. to Major General Baden-Powell, Commanding the Mafeking Frontier Forces, August 1899 to May 1900. He was also Baden-Powell's A.D.C. after that officer's promotion to Major General, South Africa, May to July 1900. He was present for the defence of Mafeking and was twice mentioned in despatches receiving the Queen's Medal with three clasps. He was promoted Lieutenant Colonel in October 1911. Lieutenant Colonel Wilson married, in 1891, Lady Sarah Isabella Augusta, sixth daughter of the seventh Duke of Marlborough, they had no children.

Captain The Honorable William Reginald Wyndham
Lincolnshire Yeomanry attached 1 Life Guards

He was killed in action 6 November, 1914, being the third son of the second Baron Leconfield. He was born 1876 and was the heir presumptive to his brother, the third Baron Leconfield. Captain Wyndham joined 17 Lancers as Second Lieutenant in March 1896, becoming Lieutenant in 1897 and Captain in July, 1901. He served in the Boer War, 1899-1900, receiving the Queen's medal with three clasps. A riding accident in 1903 caused his retirement from the army and he took a farm in East Africa. After a spell in America he returned home and became well known in Ireland as a racehorse stable owner. He was a member of the Jockey Club, to which he was elected in 1912. With the outbreak of war he made every effort to return to the army and in August 1914 he was promoted to the rank of Captain in the Lincolnshire Yeomanry. He was eventually successful in being attached to 1 Life Guards where his father and two brothers had served.

cataclysm.

Hill 60 was not noticeable, having been transformed into a mine crater, but a bridge beside it still spanned the railway cutting with a rough, red-patched arch. Water dripped and slipped down the chaotic banks into the greasy flood beneath.

There are benches and a shelter in this cemetery, and it is generally a quiet and peaceful spot. It is a cemetery that is not so huge that it daunts, and although large, is intimate enough to enable the visitor to stroll around with the register (to be found in the special container in the shelter) and spend time with these casualties of the 'war to end all wars'.

For those who are walking, continue along the track, with the railway on your left, towards Zillebeke. Drivers should proceed direct to Zillebeke Church. The walk is not particularly exciting, but it does give you a chance to look over to the right and see the ground where British troops were rushed up and took up extended formation in an attempt to retrieve the situation on Hill 60 after the German attack on 5 May 1915.

Move through the new housing in the village and turn right, heading towards the centre of Zillebeke. At the large T junction, turn left and you will see the church a hundred yards or so up the road on the right. Note that the church has two weather vanes; I am told that during the war the original was picked up and taken home as a souvenir. The church was rebuilt, and a new one placed on the tower. Many years later the original was returned, and installed at the far end of the church, though now neither weather vane can agree on the direction of the wind!

The little British section of the cemetery is not unusual in the villages of the Salient, though its high proportion of 1914 officer casualties, many of whom were members of the landed gentry has led to it being termed the ëaristocrats' cemetery.

If you are feeling energetic, cross the road and continue up it for about a kilometre. Keep your eyes peeled for a sign pointing to Tuileries British Cemetery.

This cemetery is tucked away off the road behind some houses and is situated on the site of a tile works (the Tuileries of its name). The large chimney of this works was a convenient marker for the German artillery. It was used as a burial ground in 1915, mainly in the early months of 1915, and a large number of men from such units as 1/RWK, 1/Cheshire and 2/Duke of Wellington's are buried here.

The unusual arrangement of the cemetery is due to the fact that it was

Tuileries British Cemetery, an unusually spacious cemetery.

Demarcation Stone

largely destroyed in later fighting, and therefore many of the headstones are placed along the walls - they are known to have been buried here, but where their bodies are precisely in the cemetery now is unknown. It makes for a different feel to the cemetery, with its large expanse of greenery.

Return to Zillebeke and head back the way you came, though this time staying on the road. To the left of the railway line, on the Zillebeke side, was Zillebeke Halt, frequently mentioned in war diaries and accounts. On the other side of the road and some distance into the field was Manor Farm, and beyond that the great expanse of Zillebeke Lake.

Proceed over the railway line until the road meets the junction with Verbranden Road. Note the demarcation stone, marking the limit of the German advance, on the traffic island. This particular stone has got a British helmet on the top and British equipment on its surrounds.

Turn right and take the first turning left; at the bottom of the road, about three hundred yards away, you will see the blue gates of a farm, thereby

Lieut. Colonel G A Hamilton, The Master of Belhaven.

gratifyingly retaining the link with its Great War (and present) name, Blauwepoort Farm. The cemetery may be seen to the left of the farm buildings. Whilst walking down to the cemetery, look to the half right and note the beginnings of Messines Ridge (a large red and white radio mast is a helpful guide) and before that, just visible, is Bedford House Cemetery. Looking to the left and scanning across from there rightwards, you can clearly see the valley which the Master of Belhaven called Blauwepoort Valley. At this point I would particularly urge readers to get hold of the book based on his diaries and letters (still in print, *The Master of Belhaven,* by the same publishers as this work). It is probably among the ten most impressive personal Great War recollection books printed, complete with helpful (if occasionally rather faint) sketches. He was a gunner officer with a most impressive war record, killed in the early days of the German spring offensive in the Somme. The attention to detail, the powers of description and the atmosphere that it evokes makes this a vital book in the understanding of the war. The book includes much about his time here - at one stage his battery was based on Blauwepoort Farm - and in Larch Wood dugouts, in particular in the time around 1917.

When you get to the cemetery, look back up the road and see how the Verbranden road is relatively high up and cuts off the view from the Hill 60 side. Small variations of height, in a landscape so flat as this, have a very disproportionate effect on views.

Blauwepoort Farm Cemetery was begun by French troops in November 1914 (they were *chasseurs alpins* - rather out of their training element - and

Panorama from Blauwepoort Farm.

BATTLE WOOD

VERSBRANDEN ROAD

Blauwepoort Farm. The farmgates are still painted blue.

were the soldiers who were forced off Hill 60 by the Germans). It was used by the British between February 1915 to February 1916. There are ninety eight men buried here, of whom eight are unknown. It is a spacious cemetery, and a battlefield one; ie it was created at the time of the fighting, on the battlefield, and no new graves were brought here after the war ended. This was probably because it was well off the road, and the access in the immediate post war period was probably very poor (compared, say, to the railway line going past Larch Wood, which operated on a tram way basis up to there even at the height of the fighting). All of those buried here are men who fought at Hill 60, with a large number, in particular, from 5/South Staffs and 6/North Staffs.

It is a rarely visited cemetery, and does not deserve this fate. It is another good spot to stop, reflect and even have one's picnic lunch.

Return to the main road and turn left, proceed across the railway line and almost immediately afterwards you will come to **Railway Dugouts Burial Ground (Transport Farm).** This is a massive cemetery, stretching over a lot of ground, with over 2,200 buried here. Burials were begun in April 1915 and reached their height in 1916 and 1917 when there were Advanced Dressing Stations in the dugouts and adjacent (and now rebuilt) Transport Farm. The graves were scattered about, and a large number were destroyed in shell fire in connection with the Messines Offensive; 258 known graves were destroyed by this artillery fire. Amongst those buried here is young Frederick Youens VC.

The Railway Dugouts were adjacent; my grandfather would have numbered himself amongst those who considered themselves very fortunate to have the benefit of their cover when his battalion, 7/Leicesters, took shelter here during the Battle of the Lys in April 1918.

The cemetery has an individual characteristic, despite its size, helped by the immediacy of the battlefield, the physical symbols of the war, the Railway Dugouts and the British bunker in the field opposite, and Transport Farm itself. The regimental history of 6/South Staffs notes the extra comfort provided by the pond by Transport Farm,

> *in the cool waters of which the men were wont, during lulls in the whizz-banging, to bathe themselves, and even attempt the pleasures of fishing! Many a fish must owe its life to the sudden arrival of a German shell, and the necessary withdrawal of the fishermen.*

BLAUWEPOORT CEMETERY   KEMMEL

Railway Dugouts (Transport Farm) Cemetery.

Return to the road and to Zillebeke, but instead of turning left towards the church, press on along Knoll Road, along which many hundreds of troops would have tramped en route to the line at Zwarteleen. Just where the road turns left, towards Hill 60, on the left hand side, was the approximate site of Private Warner's VC action.

Proceed to your car.

You might like to take a short drive to see roughly where Youens got his VC.

Return to Knoll Road and turn right, the road to Zandvoorde (Tenbrielen, the German billeting village, was beyond this - it is now known as Timbrielje). Shortly after the wood on your right clears, there is a turning on the right towards Hollebeke. At this point look into the fields on your left: this was the area of 13/DLI and the German lines after the Battle of Messines and where Youens was both wounded initially, then came out to save the situation and received his fatal wounding.

Exhausted, return to Ypres via Shrapnel Corner and the Lille Gate and have a good meal and a health giving drink!

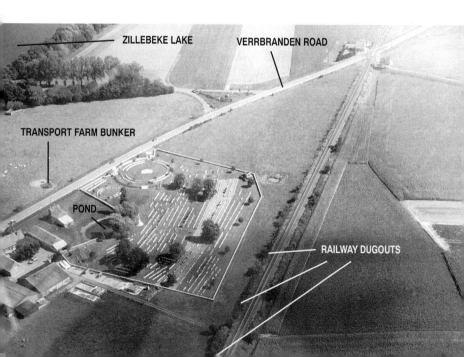

Further Reading

There are numerous guides to the battlefields of the Salient. The traditional starting point for the new visitor is a copy of the late Rose E Coombs, *Before Endeavours Fade*, which is readily available in the outlets, such as the Cloth Hall Museum, in the area, and in the bigger bookshops in the UK.

John Giles' *The Ypres Salient Then and Now* was the first of the books in recent times to go to this particular format. It provides a good read and some detailed descriptions of particular areas though, alas, progress has meant that some of the places featured have suffered at the hands of the developers.

More recently, Pen and Sword Books have brought out Major and Mrs Holt's *Battlefield Guide to the Ypres Salient*, an excellent and full tour and explanation of the battlefield. It is accompanied by a most helpful map, which is provided separate from the book.

Paul Reed's, *Walking the Salient,* takes the hardier traveller on a number of walks around the Salient. In the same Battleground Europe series there is also Peter Oldham's *Messines Ridge*, whilst some of the action to the north of Hill 60 is covered in my *Sanctuary Wood and Hooge.*

Of the first hand accounts of the fighting here, I would most particularly recommend *A Sergeant-Major's War: From Hill 60 to the Somme,* Ernest Shephard, edited by Bruce Rossor. This is the diary of a soldier who fought here in the trying days of May 1915. Another first class read, and not just for what he has to say about Hill 60, is *The War Diary of the Master of Belhaven*, reprinted and available from Pen and Sword Books.

The battles of 1915 are still relatively poorly covered, though Lyn Macdonald's *1915 The Death of Innocence* has gone some way to filling the gap. A good history (any history?) is still awaited for the Battle of Messines.

Hill 60: The Index